On the Pragmatics of Soc

On the Pragmatics of Social Interaction

Preliminary Studies in the Theory of Communicative Action

Jürgen Habermas

Translated by Barbara Fultner

Polity

This translation Copyright © 2001 Massachusetts Institute of Technology

Though substantially revised, this translation is based on Jeremy Shapiro's original translation of the Gauss Lectures when they were delivered at Princeton.

The lectures and essays in this volume appeared in German in Jürgen Habermas, *Vorstudien und Ergänzungen zur Theorie des kommunikativen Handelns*, © 1984 Suhrkamp Verlag, Frankfurt am Main, Germany.

First published in 2001 by Polity Press in association with Blackwell Publishing Ltd.

First published in paperback 2003.

Editorial office:
Polity Press
65 Bridge street
Cambridge CB2 1UR, UK

Marketing and production:
Blackwell Publishing Ltd
108 Cowley Road
Oxford OX4 1JF, UK

ISBN: 0-7456 2551-7
ISBN: 0-7456 3219-X (pb)

A catalogue record for this book is available from the British Library.

Typeset in New Baskerville by Wellington Graphics, Westwood, Massachusetts, USA.
Printed and bound in Great Britain by Athenaeum Press Ltd., Gateshead.

For further information on Polity, visit our website: www.polity.co.uk

Contents

Contents

Translator's Introduction

Philosophy in the twentieth century, in both its analytic and continental traditions, has been shaped by what has come to be known as "the linguistic turn." Be it in metaphysics, epistemology, or value theory, philosophy of language has become a keystone of conceptual analysis. Most profoundly perhaps, the linguistic turn has affected the conception and understanding of reason. It is no longer possible today to defend the universal validity of a transcendent, objective reason, nor can language be regarded any longer as a neutral tool at reason's disposal. The role of this movement in critical theory is due in large measure to the work of Jürgen Habermas. And yet, in an increasingly postmodern era, Habermas has remained a defender of modernity. While the reason of the enlightenment has come under general attack, he continues to endorse its emancipatory potential, albeit in the altered form of a "postmetaphysical" reason that is always situated in contexts of interaction. Habermas locates the roots of rationality in the structures of everyday communication such that the critical power of reason is immanent in ordinary language from the start. The aim of his intersubjectivist account of "communicative reason" is to displace both subjectivist accounts that cling to Cartesian conceptions of monological selfhood and objectivist accounts that ignore the agent's perspective entirely.

The essays and lectures collected in this volume explain why Habermas considers a linguistic turn to be necessary, how he thinks it is to be worked out, and what he takes its implications to be. They address questions concerning the nature of social interaction and its connection to communication, and they trace the implications for developing an adequate social theory. They will be of interest not only to readers who have followed Habermas's intellectual development but also to those looking for an introduction to his theory of communicative action. More generally, philosophers of language will find in these essays a host of original ideas on the relationship between language and society.

Since its publication in 1981, Habermas's *The Theory of Communicative Action*[1] has been widely acclaimed for its contribution to philosophy and social theory. However, its two volumes are daunting, not only for reasons of length, but owing to the breadth of its subject matter and the denseness of its argumentation. The essays and lectures in the present volume provide a less arduous route to understanding the theory behind that larger work. They are a partial translation of *Vorstudien und Ergänzungen zur Theorie des kommunikativen Handelns,* which was published in 1984 and contains not only preliminary studies leading up to the fully developed theory of communicative action, but also several essays that complement *The Theory of Communicative Action* in important respects. The first part of this volume, "Reflections on the Linguistic Foundation of Sociology," formed the text of the Gauss Lectures that Habermas delivered at Princeton in 1971.[2] These lectures are driven by the same theoretical aim that underlies *The Theory of Communicative Action,* namely, the attempt to ground a theory of society on the foundations of communicative rationality. They provide a largely self-contained account of the philosophical motivations behind the theory of communicative action as well as an elucidation of its theoretical grounding in what Habermas called first *universal* and later *formal pragmatics.* The presentation of the issues here is more accessible than in *The Theory of Communicative Action* precisely because Habermas is occupied with laying out the general parameters of his project and situating it relative to other theories of society. Moreover, he discusses certain issues here, such as "systematically distorted communication," that he has not addressed in the same detail again. In short, these "preparatory studies" offer important aids to understanding his mature philosophy and social theory.

Habermas's interest in the theory of language and meaning has always been motivated by his work in social theory and the theory of action. Throughout his career, he has sought to integrate philosophy and empirical social research, in particular to illuminate the foundations of social theory while remaining faithful to the methods and results of empirical inquiry. His primary concern has been with problems of social action and action coordination, and with the use of communicative reason as a means of addressing such problems. The resultant theory of communicative action accords a foundational role to linguistic communication, inasmuch as communicative action, as Habermas understands it, is action oriented toward reaching mutual understanding, which he regards as the inherent telos of language. In acting communicatively, an agent seeks to reach an understanding with another about something in the world. The goal of formal pragmatics is to identify the universal conditions and presuppositions of such processes of reaching mutual understanding in language. The terms "universal" and "formal" draw attention to key claims of this theory: (1) the presuppositions it identifies are unavoidable if communication is to take place at all; (2) it is not concerned with the pragmatics of particular speech situations but with a general "species" competence; and (3) it reconstructs formal rather than substantive conditions of reaching mutual understanding. For Habermas, the structures of communicative rationality are to be found in the formal structures of speech; rational principles of deliberation are implicit in the structure of ordinary language communication. Thus language, reason, and action are inherently intermeshed.

The Gauss Lectures mark the beginning of Habermas's appropriation of speech act theory and contain the first formulation of his formal pragmatics.[3] His central concern is with explicating the "binding and bonding" force of speech acts, which underwrites what he calls their action-coordinating power. For this purpose, speech act theory offers several advantages. First, it focuses on *utterances* rather than sentences and thus aims to be a *pragmatic* theory of meaning, rather than a semantic theory completely abstracted from contexts of use. Second, it gives formal recognition to nonassertoric uses of language and to that extent departs from typically "cognitivist" approaches to semantics. Third, speech act theory analytically separates a speech act's propositional from its illocutionary component, which makes it possible to distinguish between what speakers say about the world and the intersubjective relations they establish in doing so.[4]

What originally prompted Habermas to apply this linguistic approach to social theory was his desire to steer a course between two dominant paradigms in social science, neither of which can provide a satisfactory model. The first is the objectivist paradigm, which assimilates the social to the natural sciences. It examines social situations entirely from the external perspective of an observer looking for patterns of behavior. This approach is characteristically uninterested in *agency* or in what a given behavior means from the engaged perspective of the agents involved, and as a result, it fails to provide an adequate account of intersubjectivity. A prime example of this type of approach is classical behaviorism. The second paradigm is the subjectivist, which adopts the point of view of participants and construes society as a meaningfully structured whole. This approach is interested in intentional actions rather than mere behavior, it acknowledges the centrality of interpretation, and it views subjects as implicated in constituting their worlds. However, it too fails to provide an adequate account of intersubjectivity, not because it ignores the perspective of the agent, but because it gets caught in the monological perspective of a Cartesian subject. And that perspective makes it hard to see how meaningful societal structures can be formed at all. In other words, the subjectivistic approach has difficulty explaining how it is possible to break out of the constructions of a solitary constituting subject into a genuine social reality. Nonetheless, the connection between constitution and interpretation provides Habermas with the opening he needs to give critical theory a linguistic turn: an adequate social theory must account for the fact that subjects in interaction encounter the world and one another as *meaningfully* structured.

Habermas offers a third—communicative—paradigm that takes intersubjectivity into account from the start and regards language as its proper medium. The differences between the subjectivist and objectivist paradigms turn on their respective decisions to allow or reject "meaning" as a basic, irreducible concept. In Habermas's view, to understand the nature of intersubjectivity, we need to understand how agents interacting with one another arrive at the same interpretations of their situation; in this respect, intersubjectivity is grounded in sameness of meaning. Habermas regards communication in language as the paradigm case of achieving such "identity of meaning" and thus holds that linguistic normativity cannot be reduced to mere behavior in the sense of the objectivist paradigm. To distance himself from the subjectivist paradigm, Habermas goes on to argue that the normativity of meaning must be based on the intersubjective (rather than merely subjective) validity of a rule. Thus, intersubjectivity is to be explained on the model of how two different individuals are able to use a term with one and the same meaning.

That interlocutors succeed in assigning the same meanings to their actions and circumstances attests to their mastery of what Habermas calls "communicative competence." On this view, if we can delineate the structure of communicative competence, we will also have captured the structure of communicative rationality. Habermas's formal pragmatics aims to provide a rational reconstruction of this competence, that is, to transform an implicit knowledge, a know-how, into a "second-level know-that."[5] This is not to say, of course, that a speaker actually has representations of the reconstructed knowledge "in the head." Her know-how is pretheoretic: a skill or mastery of a practice in the Wittgensteinian sense. Subjects capable of speech and action have acquired a tacit mastery of rule-governed practices that enable them to reach a mutual understanding with one another about the world. Successful communication requires, then, that the rules constituting such communicative competence be valid intersubjectively.

Habermas uses Husserl, Sellars, and Wittgenstein as foils for his own account. The subjectivist and objectivist paradigms are represented by Edmund Husserl and Wilfrid Sellars respectively. In *The Cartesian Meditations*, Husserl explicitly sets himself the task of reconstructing intersubjectivity from a subjectivist starting point. (The tradition of interpretive sociology initiated by Alfred Schütz is rooted in this Husserlian enterprise.) Habermas argues that Husserl's phenomenology of consciousness fails in the end to establish the intersubjectivity of a community of transcendental egos, and so he turns to Sellars. Sellars's approach is initially promising because he wants to model intentionality and the structure of thought on the structure of language: He takes a linguistic turn within the philosophy of mind. However, his understanding of language, according to Habermas, is essentially objectivist. That is, speakers come to mean the same things by the same words because they respond similarly to their environment and mutually observe each other's responses from a monological, third-person perspective rather than from a dialogical second-person perspective. They are "monological language users" with a full, intentional (inner) life of beliefs and desires, but lacking any interpersonal relationships. But monological language that cannot be used for purposes of communicating with others, Habermas argues, is not really language at all. Thus, in different ways, Husserl and Sellars both presuppose rather than account for the existence of intersubjectivity.

It is no accident that Habermas's argument against Sellars is reminiscent of Wittgenstein's private-language argument. Sameness of meaning is grounded in the validity of rules, and Habermas, following Wittgenstein, argues that a subject cannot follow rules in isolation. If someone is following a rule, it must be at least in principle possible for someone else to check whether she is following that rule correctly; one person's rule-following behavior is, in other words, subject to evaluation and criticism by another. This precludes any monological account of rule-following, for it presupposes that different people have the same competence and are mutually capable of assessing each other's performance.[6] Wittgenstein emphasized that meaning is a matter of use and that words and sentences are used in interaction with others; his "use theory of meaning" was in this sense inherently pragmatic and intersubjective. As action and language are intimately interwoven, to understand an utterance is to grasp its role in a language game, that is, to understand it as a move in a rule-governed, interpersonal activity. Thus being able to engage in a language game presupposes sharing a form of life with one's interlocutors. The rules constitutive of such language games are not stipulated arbitrarily, but have the status of conventions, a topic to which I shall return below. Habermas elaborates on Wittgenstein's account in two ways. First, he aims to develop a theory of the structures of intersubjectivity: Though Wittgenstein's language games clearly suppose dialogical relationships among participants in interaction, he does not analyze these relationships as such. Second, Habermas wants to do more justice than Wittgenstein did to the fact that language refers to the world.

The early Wittgenstein attempted to elaborate a purely cognitive language, the prime function of which was to represent the totality of facts that make up the world. The later Wittgenstein aborted that attempt because, in Habermas's terms, he discovered communicative language use(s). In other words, he came to realize that language can be used for all sorts of purposes other than cognitive ones and, according to Habermas, henceforth mistakenly downplayed the importance of the cognitive use altogether. By contrast, Habermas maintains that reaching mutual understanding requires a speaker and hearer to operate at two levels: the level of intersubjectivity on which they speak with one another, and the level of objects or states of affairs about which they communicate. His discussion here is arguably the best, most extensive elucidation of his conception of the "double structure of speech." He makes it clear that the two uses of language are *interdependent*. "A communicative theory of society must do justice to the double cognitive-communicative structure of speech" (p. 64). This dual structure underlies the reflexive character of language: Natural languages can function as their own meta-languages, as Donald Davidson, for example, has also pointed out. According to Habermas, we cannot communicate about things or states of affairs in the world without also "meta-communicating" about what we are doing or how we are using the content of what we are saying. It is here that speech act theory enters the picture. Every speech act takes the form Mp, where M expresses the illocutionary force of the utterance (the communicative dimension) and p expresses its propositional content (the cognitive dimension) about which mutual understanding is to be reached. In this sense, all speech acts have a cognitive and a communicative dimension.

Habermas's key move in linking communicative rationality with a theory of meaning is to connect the theory of meaning with a theory of argumentation and justification. There is, as he puts it, a "validity basis" to speech; all speech acts carry an implicit commit-ment to justification, to giving reasons that back one's claims. When we use speech acts to communicate with one another, we move, as Robert Brandom has recently reminded us, in "the space of giving and asking for reasons."[7] Or, as Habermas puts it, every speech act raises certain claims to validity that are open to being challenged and defended with reasons. The illocutionary component of an utter-ance expresses validity claims a speaker raises in performing speech acts. Habermas initially identifies four such claims: intelligibility, truth, normative rightness, and sincerity or truthfulness. That is, in making an utterance, a speaker simultaneously raises the claims that what she says is intelligible, that the propositional content of what she says is true, that she is making the utterance in the appropriate social context, and that she is speaking truthfully. Following on this, Habermas classifies speech acts into four types, each of which corre-sponds to one of the four validity claims: communicatives (e.g., speaking, asking, replying), constatives (e.g., reporting, asserting, claiming), regulatives (e.g., ordering, requesting, demanding, re-minding), and expressives (e.g., knowing, thinking, fearing, hoping, wishing). Communicative speech acts are used to make explicit the nature of an utterance itself. In constative speech acts, speakers rep-resent states of affairs in the objective world and refer to something in that world. In performing regulative speech acts, speakers estab-lish intersubjective relationships with interlocutors and thus relate to a social world. In expressive speech acts, speakers refer to things in their subjective world by making public intentions, desires, or other private states or occurrences. In *The Theory of Communicative Action,* the number of validity claims is reduced to three; intelligibility drops out, leaving truth, normative rightness, and sincerity.[8]

Communicative action takes place against a background consen-sus that it renews and develops. When communicative interaction is proceeding smoothly, interlocutors make what they are saying intelli-gible to one another, grant what they are saying to be true (i.e., they assume the referential expressions they are using pick out objects to which the attributes they predicate of them actually apply), recog-nize the rightness of the norm that the speech act claims to fulfill, and don't doubt each other's sincerity. In short, they mutually accept *communicative rationality*

communicative competence.
communicative unbegacha

the validity of the claims being raised. In this "normal" case, a speaker uses expressions such that the hearer understands the speaker as the speaker wants to be understood, she formulates propositional contents such that they represent experiences or facts, she expresses her intentions (sincerely), and she performs speech acts such that they conform to recognized norms of accepted self-images. At the same time, participants in communicative action are assumed to be prepared to reach mutual understanding—that is, their attitude is communicative rather than strategic (oriented toward realizing one's own ends). As such, they are assumed to be accountable, that is, capable of justifying their actions and expressions. Accountability thus refers to a general presumption of rationality, cashed out in terms of one's readiness to justify the claims one raises. Because, normally, in raising validity claims, a speaker takes on the warrant to make good on them, formal pragmatics as a theory of "communicative rationality" can serve as a foundation for a *critical* theory. As a speaker can be called upon to justify the claims raised in her utterances, the burden of justification and the possibility of critique are built into the very structure of language and communication.

When the consensus underlying smoothly functioning communicative interaction breaks down and the flow of the language game is interrupted, particular claims to validity may be thematized. To redeem problematic claims to truth or to normative rightness, we must resort to a level of argumentation that Habermas calls *discourse*, through which we seek to attain a *rational* consensus on these claims. But how are speakers able to distinguish a true (or rational) from a false (or merely contingent) consensus? Note that we routinely assume, as a matter of fact, that we are able to do so, and that, in this sense, speech is fundamentally rational. To model the assumptions built into the ideal of rational discourse, Habermas introduces the notion of the *ideal speech situation*. The ideal speech situation is subject only to the "unforced force of the better argument"; it is devoid of all other constraints. All interlocutors are equally entitled to make assertions, raise questions and objections, or provide justifications for their positions. And all express their true intentions. It is crucial to remember that discourses *as a matter of fact* usually do not manifest the conditions of the ideal speech situation, but the model can serve

Foucault
force

RA, DM dependent on speech acts cl are justifiable with reasons that back claims validity basis.

as a standard in identifying deviations from the ideal of rational
consensus.

The question of whence the justifications for thematized validity
claims are drawn brings us to the notion of the lifeworld, which is
complementary to that of communicative action. The lifeworld provides a context of relevance within which communicative actions
(and actors) are "always already" situated. As such, it always remains
in the background, standing "at the backs" of participants in communication, as it were. It cannot be transcended: Speakers and actors
cannot act by placing themselves outside of it. It has, on the contrary,
a transcendental character insofar as it functions itself as a condition
of possibility for communicative action. In this sense, it functions as a
background of mutual intelligibility. Intersubjectively shared, it
makes possible the smooth functioning of everyday communicative
action. In general, speakers do not have explicit but only tacit knowledge of it; nonetheless, the lifeworld provides communicative actors
with a shared stock of taken-for-granted interpretations on which
they can draw in trying to understand others. In discourse, elements
of this implicit knowledge can be rendered explicit in order to redeem validity claims that have been challenged. This connection between universal pragmatics and the lifeworld is discussed in the
fourth Gauss Lecture, where Habermas defends the linguistic turn in
phenomenology and suggests that universal pragmatics aims to elucidate basic structures of the lifeworld. Thus we can see that he early
on conceived communicative action and lifeworld as complementary, a connection he later strengthened and elaborated in *The Theory of Communicative Action.*

Of special note is Habermas's discussion of truth in the Gauss Lectures, for truth claims enjoy paradigmatic status as validity claims
(p. 86). When we raise a truth claim, we use language cognitively.
And Habermas's discussion of cognitive language use in the Gauss
Lectures focuses on questions of reference and perception—elements that are not emphasized in his subsequent articulations of formal pragmatics. When attributing a property to an object, he claims,
a speaker presupposes that the object exists and that the proposition
she asserts is true. That is, she assumes that the subject expression
has a referent and that the predicate can be correctly applied to it.

Habermas here endorses a description theory of reference. Interestingly, he also states that our experience is in the first instance sensory and only in the second instance communicative (p. 79). In light of recent criticisms to the effect that he needs a theory of reference to avoid some form of linguistic idealism, the Gauss discussion is therefore important.[9]

It is also important because it contains an early treatment of the so-called *consensus theory of truth,* which emerges from Habermas's account of the discursive redemption or vindication of validity claims. As we have seen, a claim is discursively vindicated if rational consensus is reached concerning its validity, and the meaning of truth, according to Habermas, is explicated by specifying the conditions under which validity claims can (or could) be vindicated. All of this suggests an epistemic conception of truth as what is rationally agreed upon under ideal conditions. The interest of the "consensus theory of truth," however, lies not so much in what it says about the nature of truth, as in what it says about how we reach agreement on claims to truth. Thus it is not so much a theory of *truth* as a theory of *justification.* And in fact, Habermas has since abandoned an epistemic conception of truth and has developed this conception of rational consensus primarily in the context of his theory of discourse ethics, which he developed after the completion of *The Theory of Communicative Action.*[10]

While the Gauss Lectures focus on truth as a dimension of validity, "Intentions, Conventions, and Linguistic Interactions" (1976), an essay more explicitly located within the philosophy of action, focuses on the validity of social norms and examines the conceptual interconnections between rules, conventions, norm-governed action, and intentionality. Rather than establishing the need for a theory of communicative action on the grounds that other theories have failed to provide adequate accounts of intersubjectivity, Habermas is here concerned to demonstrate the need for a theory of action that is intersubjective. The concept of communicative action is to account for intentional action, that is, action caused by internal intentional states (in Brentano's sense) of the agent, as well as for norm-conforming action or behavior in the sense of action in accordance with external rules. The essay aims at developing a concept of communicative action (or, as he puts it here, interaction mediated through interpretation) that incorporates both intentional and norm-governed action. Habermas concludes that the two models of intentional and norm-governed action that he discusses are complementary, and that linguistic communication can be seen as constitutive for both. But he does not advocate assimilating or reducing social to linguistic theory. Indeed, he argues against taking language as a paradigm for rule-following, or assimilating semantic and social conventions and taking the former as paradigmatic of the latter, since this would obscure the crucial distinction between communicative and strategic action. Rather, he conceives conventions "in the sense of valid—that is, intersubjectively recognized-norms" as a subset of rules of action in general. The latter includes rules of instrumental action and strategic rules as well.

The duality of cognitive and noncognitive orientations continues to play a role in this essay as well. Habermas draws an analytic distinction between two types of intentionality, one referring to a cognitive relation to a world of objects, the other referring to the stance a subject adopts toward the propositional content she is expressing. Intentional action can be understood on the model of teleological action, in that the agent has a goal that she intends to accomplish and which thus functions as a cause of her actions. When we examine intentional action with a view to the agent's cognitive relation to the world, it is possible—up to a point—to understand this relation monologically. That is, we can consider her as an individual in isolation from others and independently of the culture in which she lives. But as soon as we try to give an account of how the agent comes to have the goals she has, this model begins to break down. For her goals depend on her desires and other intentional states, which in turn result from what Habermas calls her "need interpretations." These in turn are a function of the agent's cultural values and norms, and this means that intentional action cannot be accounted for monologically. Rather, our account of need interpretations requires looking at how subjects interact in accordance with mutually recognized norms and values, and this establishes a nexus between intersubjective cultural traditions and individual needs.

One of the negative consequences of starting from the teleological means-ends model is that values and motives of action are represented as private needs and wants—the most serious flaw of an empiricist ethics, in Habermas's view. But if a person's motives are to be intelligible to others, need interpretations must be intersubjective, although their intelligibility does not yet constitute a normatively binding standard. An intelligible motive is not yet a justification; the latter requires reasons that all can share: "To say that a norm is valid is to say that it claims to express a universalizable interest and to deserve the consent of all those affected" (p. 122). This formulation anticipates Habermas's subsequent formulation of the principle of universalizability of discourse ethics. More importantly, however, these relatively early writings show the deep connection between the universalizability of interests and their origin in intersubjectivity. Insofar as our wants and needs always appear under some interpretation, they presuppose a community that has a language containing evaluative expressions, which in turn are rooted in an intersubjectively shared tradition of cultural values. These values become normatively binding when there is a consensus that is reproduced in language and sedimented in the form of conventions.

Conventions, of course, are commonly appealed to in order to explain how we understand one another. Habermas does not presuppose that there simply *are* such conventions that make mutual understanding possible any more than he presupposes that there simply *are* subjects who abide by them (let alone stipulate them). Instead, relying on G. H. Mead's analyses, he offers a developmental account of how such conventions are established as normative expectations presupposed in speech acts.[11] Once we accept that both having intentions and acting in accordance with norms presuppose linguistic interaction, we can understand how subject formation is the result of linguistic interaction, how we are socialized in and through communicative interaction.

IMPT.+

Finally, the essay "Reflection on Communicative Pathology" (1974) seeks to address the question of deviant processes of socialization—a topic that any developmental account of interactive competence must address—and contains an analysis of the formal conditions of

PTO.

systematically distorted communication. Habermas's guiding assumption here is that the development of interactive competence is connected to the development of internal mechanisms for controlling behavior, but that these two developments are distinct (since moral judgments and actual behavior in conflict resolution do not coincide). His analysis stresses the connection between linguistic communication and ego development: "Communicative action is the medium of socialization" (p. 131). Picking up on a theme mentioned above, this essay establishes the connection between subjectivity and intersubjectivity by showing that a subject's intentions are socially, that is, intersubjectively, structured.

Habermas wants to show that both social and individual pathologies can be analyzed in terms of disturbances in interactive competence. Such an account, however, presupposes a model of *undisturbed* or *normal* communication and interaction in the terms of his formal pragmatics. On this approach the notion of normalcy is not determined by any particular culture, nor is it a statistical norm; it is rather a culturally invariant normative notion.

Habermas has been criticized for presenting too idealized an account of communication, particularly owing to his notion of the ideal speech situation. This last essay shows that he is very much attuned to the empirical vagaries of communication. In claiming that the validity basis of speech has transcendental status, Habermas certainly does not mean to imply that we cannot deviate from the conditions of normal communication; otherwise, we would not have to explicate the *normative* basis of speech. The conditions of possible communication are thus not transcendental in the same sense as, say, Kant's transcendental intuitions of space and time qua conditions of possible perception. Nonetheless, the formal presuppositions underlying communication are, according to Habermas, *unavoidable.* Moreover, as such they function somewhat like *regulative ideals* in the Kantian sense. They are not inviolable, but in cases where the internal organization of speech is violated, the patterns of communication are pathologically distorted. We have already seen that interlocutors may challenge the validity claims raised by others and thereby prompt communication shifts from action to discourse. It is also possible that the claims to intelligibility, truth, rightness, or sincerity are continually suspended or flawed without prompting such a shift. If this happens, the result is systematically distorted communication. The kind of violation of the universal presuppositions of communication that leads to systematic distortion is not the result of a lack of competence in the language, a misconception of the level of discussion, or a retreat from communicative to strategic action. These all involve a cessation of communicative action, whereas in the cases that Habermas has in mind, communicative action continues in spite of the violation of its formal presuppositions. The strongest cases of systematic distortion are those in which the speaking subjects themselves are unaware of their violation of communicative presuppositions, such as when a competent speaker expresses herself unintelligibly without realizing it, when one spouse deceives herself about her feelings for the other, or when a speaker thinks she is acting in accordance with social norms but is actually violating them.

Ideally, the rejection of a validity claim leads to discourse, in which the speaker seeks to justify the claims she is making; or the speaker shows by her actions that she is sincere. But this does not happen in cases of distorted communication that stem from conflicts that cannot be quite suppressed yet must not become openly manifest— because, for example, they threaten the identity or self-understanding of one or more interlocutors. This sort of situation results in a kind of paradox of systematic distortion of communication, for the very validity claims that are being violated "serve to keep up the appearance of consensual action" (p. 155).

This discussion makes clear that the idealizations required by this model of communication may fail. However, the idealized model allows for a systematic understanding of the different *sorts* of failure and provides the norms or standards for *criticizing* them.

As the empirical literature upon which Habermas draws in this discussion indicates, systematic distortions connected with subject-formation occur particularly often within families. Not only is this a context in which people's identities are formed and confirmed, it is a context in which a particularly high premium is placed on communicative rather than strategic action. On the one hand, families are expected to function as units; on the other hand, the needs and wants of individuals have to be met within the family structure. Thus there is a tension and potential conflict between the orientation toward mutual understanding and the orientation toward individual need satisfaction. Failure to resolve such conflicts explicitly can lead to systematically distorted communication, in which members employ different strategies for maintaining or producing a "pseudo-consensus." They may seek to safeguard an endangered consensus and prevent challenges to it by, for instance, interrupting or breaking off conversation, reformulating a disagreement as an agreement, falsely reciprocating another's action, or—in the most extreme case that threatens the very intelligibility of their utterances and actions inasmuch as incoherence violates the norms of rationality—behaving inconsistently. The notion of systematically distorted communication evidently introduces a third option between the successful completion of a speech act and what J. L. Austin terms a "misfire" in which the speech act itself fails.

Habermas links a family's potential for conflict to power relations, claiming that a "family's ability to solve . . . problems stands in an inverse relation to its internal potential for conflict. The latter in turn is a function of the distribution of power" (p. 161). He does not, however, suggest that a healthy family must succeed in transcending power relations. Rather, he allows for a "healthy" distribution of power, which, nevertheless, is connected to an "asymmetrical distribution of opportunities" for gratification. Once again, there is a clear recognition that empirical circumstances—even in communicatively structured contexts—diverge significantly from the ideal speech situation.

While these lectures and essays provide a good introduction to the theory of communicative action, they are also transitional in nature: They form a bridge between Habermas's work of the 1960s and that of the 1980s. His linguistic turn was initially motivated by the conviction that a critical social theory required a sound methodological and epistemological foundation: hence the project of providing a linguistic grounding for sociology. However, the project of developing a comprehensive theory of rationality, which is what the theory of communicative action in effect attempts, cannot be carried out merely from the methodological perspective of finding an alternative to objectivist and subjectivist social theories. Thus Habermas soon found it necessary to develop an account of the presuppositions of action oriented toward reaching understanding independently of an account of the transcendental presuppositions of social-scientific knowledge.[12] This helps explain why the distinction between cognitive and communicative language use, which is so central in the Gauss Lectures, becomes less prominent in his subsequent formulations of the theory of communicative action.[13]

At the same time, while Habermas has been working out a complex theory of action, he has also elaborated his conception of speech act theory and of formal pragmatics to serve as the basis for a social theory of meaning. Since the writing of the Gauss Lectures, he has developed a systematic classification scheme for theories of meaning, in which he distinguishes formal semantics, intentionalist semantics, and use theories of meaning. In his view, each of these focuses on but one of the three functions of language that an adequate theory of meaning must incorporate. As we saw, in communicating, we represent facts about the world, we express our subjective states, and we interact with others; and these three functions correspond to the three validity claims of truth, sincerity, and rightness that formal pragmatics analyzes.[14] In his recent work, in addition to speech act theory, Habermas also draws on Michael Dummett's assertibilist semantics, according to which the meaning of a sentence (or utterance) is given by the conditions under which it is acceptable to hearers. Developing this aspect of formal pragmatics once again underscores the aspects of rationality and intersubjectivity; for to say that understanding an utterance is knowing the conditions under which it is acceptable entails that a speaker-hearer does not fully understand a given utterance unless she knows what reasons could be offered to back up the claims raised in the utterance. And construed in this way, acceptability conditions cannot be determined independently of an intersubjective practice of argumentation and justification.

Habermas has recently returned to some of the themes adumbrated in the early 1970s. One of these is the question of the nature of truth, as I indicated above. Another is the distinction between communicative and noncommunicative language use.[15] Yet the views articulated in these early works are not only relevant to Habermas's current thought; they bear on contemporary philosophical discussions more broadly. Within Anglo-American philosophy, there has been a resurgence of interest in pragmatics and in social theories of meaning that do justice to the intersubjectivity of social interaction. A prime example is Robert Brandom's *Making It Explicit,* which is an elaborate working out of a semantic theory based on social practices and, in particular, practices of justification. On Brandom's view, semantics is based on the giving of and asking for reasons: To give the meaning of a sentence is to articulate the conditions under which its assertion is justified, which is to articulate a web of justificatory relations. However, unlike Habermas, Brandom does not distinguish between irreducibly distinct types of validity claims; the focus of his analysis remains the assertion, which he continues to regard as basic. This constitutes a potential challenge to Habermas's system not only with respect to the irreducibility of the three validity claims to truth, rightness, and sincerity, but also with respect to the status of the assertion within his own framework. Given the profound influence Sellars has had on Brandom, Habermas's discussion of Sellars might also be a potentially fruitful point of engagement, with regard to both semantics and perception.[16] It would be a way of fleshing out the cognitive dimension of language and clarifying its relationship to the communicative dimension, a relationship that lies at the heart of Habermas's project.

Acknowledgments

This project would not have been possible without the help and support of others. I am indebted to Jeremy Shapiro for his excellent original translation of the Gauss Lectures, which made my own task immeasurably easier. My thanks to Harry Heft, Jonathan Maskit, Steven Vogel, Christopher Zurn, and especially Thomas McCarthy who all provided invaluable feedback on the translation and introduction. I would also like to thank Pat Davis, who transferred the original typescript of the lectures onto disk, as well as Larry Cohen and Judy Feldmann of MIT Press for their assistance. Finally, I am grateful to Jürgen Habermas for his generosity in responding to my queries.

Reflections on the Linguistic Foundation of Sociology

The Christian Gauss Lectures (Princeton University, February–March 1971)

I

Objectivist and Subjectivist Approaches to Theory Formation in the Social Sciences

There are competing theoretical approaches in the social sciences that differ not only in the kinds of problems they address and the research strategies they apply, but in their fundamental principles. They diverge in their choice of categorial frameworks and in how they conceptualize their object domain—that is, in how they define what it is they are actually studying. These differences of conceptual strategy express more deeply rooted conflicts: conflicting views of science and cognitive interests. My aim here is not to investigate and systematically expound these theoretical approaches. I intend rather to develop a particular conceptual strategy for the social sciences and to establish its theoretical plausibility and potential. I should like to begin with some comparative methodological considerations that lead to some preliminary classifications. These are to serve exclusively as a provisional delimitation of a communication theory of society. This theory does not yet exist in a satisfactory form, and I can only discuss a few issues that motivate me to consider such an approach to be fruitful.

In terms of conceptual strategy, the first decision that is of fundamental significance for a theoretical program in the social sciences is whether to admit or reject "meaning" [*Sinn*] as a primitive term. I take the paradigm of "meaning" to be the meaning [*Bedeutung*] of a word or a sentence.[1] Thus I am assuming that there are no pure or a priori speaker intentions; meaning always has or finds a symbolic expression; to attain clarity, intentions must always be able to take on symbolic form and to be expressed. This expression can be an element of a natural language or linguistically derivative (it may, for example, belong to a system of signs with which the deaf-mute or drivers in traffic communicate). The expression may also be nonverbal, that is, it may take the form of an action or of a bodily expression (a grimace or gesture), or of an artistic or musical representation. I am assuming that a meaning that is expressed nonverbally can in principle be rendered, at least approximately, in words: Whatever can be meant can be said.[2] The converse, however, does not hold. Not everything that can be said is necessarily expressible nonverbally.

If we may define "meaning" from the outset as linguistic meaning [*Sinn*], that is, with reference to the signification [*Bedeutung*] of words and sentences, then this first basic decision in conceptual strategy can be reformulated more precisely. It is in fact a metatheoretical decision as to whether linguistic communication is to be regarded as a constitutive feature of the object domain of the social sciences. The term "constitutive" means that the object domain studied by the social sciences is itself determined in terms of linguistic communication. Sometimes we describe language by using categories of observable behavior or transmissible information and explain linguistic processes in terms of learning theory. In these cases, meaningfully structured forms are taken as objects among other physical objects; the latter are described in a conceptual framework that is not specific to any language and are studied by means of empirical theories. In contrast, language is constitutive of an object domain if its categorial framework is such that meaningfully structured forms (such as persons, expressions, and institutions) can appear in it as phenomena requiring explanation. "Meaning" has the status of a primitive term in the social sciences if we use it to characterize the structure of the object domain itself, rather than just individual elements within it. I should like to clarify this first metatheoretical decision by pointing out three of its implications.

(a) Behavior versus action

Only if "meaning" is admitted as a primitive term in sociology can we distinguish action from behavior. At present I should like to set aside the prior problem of the demarcation between those observable events that we interpret as behavior and those events that we cannot interpret as behavior. The interpretive scheme that allows us to understand the motion of a body as the expression of an organism, in other words, as the movement of a living body, has not yet been satisfactorily analyzed.[3] By describing an observable motion as behavior, we ascribe it to an organism that reproduces its life by adapting to its environment. We understand it as a movement brought about by an organism. In so doing, we are assuming that there is an entity X that in some broad sense is "responsible" for this movement. In this context, of course, the category of responsibility can be used only in scare quotes, that is, with certain reservations. For an animal cannot be held responsible for its behavior in the same sense that a subject capable of speech and cognition can be held responsible for its actions. Nonetheless, we apparently derive the perspective from which we interpret motions as modes of behavior from a private modification of the pre-understanding of our own social lifeworld. I call this modification *privative* because we are capable of distinguishing behavioral responses from other events without having to appeal to the category of meaning. For that category makes it possible to differentiate between behavior that I can understand as intentional action and behavior that cannot be comprehended under this description.

I call behavior *intentional* if it is governed by norms or oriented to rules. Rules or norms do not happen like events, but hold owing to an intersubjectively recognized meaning [*Bedeutung*]. Norms have semantic content: that is, a meaning [*Sinn*] that becomes the reason or motive for behavior whenever they are obeyed by a subject to whom things are meaningful. In this case we speak of an action. The intention of an actor who orients his or her behavior to a rule corresponds to the meaning of that rule. Only this normatively guided behavior is what we call action. It is only actions that we speak of as intentional. Observable behavior fulfills a prevailing norm if and only if this behavior can be understood as produced by an acting subject who has grasped the meaning of the norm and obeyed it intentionally. Behavior that we observe over a particular period of time can de facto accord with a given norm without being norm-governed. That is why we distinguish regular behavior from rule-governed behavior, or action. We discover regularities through inductive generalizations; either they exist or they do not. In contrast, we must understand the meaning of rules; they have normative validity. We can break rules; but it is meaningless to say that regularities are violated. Rules that underlie a practice can be accepted or rejected, whereas regularities in behavior can be affirmed or denied. Naturally we can assert the existence of regularities in contexts of intentional action as much as in a chain of behavioral responses. But in the former case, we can deduce the assertion from the fact that norms are followed with specifiable probability, whereas in the latter we must base our assertion on an inductive generalization from observed behavior.

(b)   Observation versus the understanding of meaning [Sinnverstehen]

The distinction we have drawn between behavior and action leads to a further distinction between different modes of experience in which behavioral responses and actions are accessible to us. We observe behavior and behavioral regularities, whereas we understand actions. Once again it is the category of meaning that differentiates the two modes of experience. I cannot observe actions as mere behavior. For if a given behavior is to be described as an action, then I must relate features of this behavior to rules on which it is based and understand the meaning of these rules. Of course the apprehension of structures of action through the understanding of meaning rests on observations.

Let me compare two perceptual judgments or "observation statements." "I see a fly bouncing against the window" is a sentence in which I report the observation of a behavior. In contrast, "I see John returning from work" is a sentence with which I describe an "observed" action. I use the expression "to see" in the same way in both cases. For both sentences report events that the speaker claims to perceive at the time. Nevertheless, in the former case "seeing" means observing an event that can be comprehended as behavior, whereas in the latter it means understanding an action. Of course this understanding *is based on* the observation of an occurrence (the doorbell ringing, a person entering the room, etc.); but the observed behavioral elements and events are *interpreted* with reference to a structure of action. The latter consists in norms, in this case, social norms that regulate work hours and transportation to and from work. I have to be acquainted with norms of this sort and the conditions of their application in order to know when a given occurrence can be interpreted as a case in which the norm applies. "I see John returning from work" means that I understand an observed occurrence as the fulfillment of a norm: that is, as a particular action—in this case, as "returning from work." To see, observe, or perceive an action always involves understanding a norm (or the corresponding intention of the actor) and interpreting movements (or states of affairs) in the light of the norm (or intention) that is understood.

The decision whether intentional action should be admitted has methodological implications precisely with regard to the mode of experience. This can be seen at the level of problems of measurement.[4] Measurements serve to transform experience into data that meet the demands of intersubjective reliability and on the basis of which the claim to empirical validity of theoretical statements can be verified. Observations of events (and behavioral responses) can be linked with the language game of physical measurement. But there is no corresponding system of reliably inculcated basic measurement operations, such as the one available for moving bodies (or points of mass) for objects such as actions, which are accessible only through communicative experience [*sinnverstehende Erfahrung*]. In other words, observations that can be expressed in descriptive sentences of a language for things and events can be verified through recognized procedures that are reducible to physical measurement. The interpretation of the meaning of symbolic forms such as actions, which can be represented in descriptive sentences of a language for persons and expressions, cannot be reliably operationalized in analogous fashion. Until now, the measurement of symbolized meaning has depended on ad hoc procedures that in the final analysis rest on an understanding of language that remains prescientific, although it may be shaped by the discipline of hermeneutics. In principle, anyone who masters a natural language can, by virtue of communicative competence, understand an infinite number of expressions, if they are at all meaningful, and make them intelligible to others. That is, she can interpret them. Some are more practiced at this than others: Hermeneutics is an art and not a method.[5] We make use of hermeneutics, the art of interpretation, *instead* of a measurement procedure; but it is not such a procedure. The only thing that would allow for the development of basic measurement operations for meaning would be a theory of ordinary-language communication that did not merely guide and discipline the natural faculty of communicative competence, as hermeneutics does, but that could also explain it.

(c) Conventionalism versus essentialism

No matter how the problem of measuring the meaning of symbolic expressions is solved, the experiential basis of a theory of action remains distinct from that of a behaviorist theory in the strict sense. For the adequacy of a description of a meaningfully structured construct, an utterance or an action, can be tested only by reference to the knowledge of the subject who produced the expression. In many cases a subject capable of action may not be able to specify explicitly the norms according to which it orients his behavior. Nevertheless, insofar as it masters norms and can follow them, it has an implicit knowledge of rules. On the basis of this know-how it can always decide whether a given behavioral response corresponds to a known rule at all, that is, whether it can be understood as action. The subject can decide whether, in a given case, such a behavioral response accords with or deviates from a given norm, and to what extent it deviates from an underlying norm. The situation is similar with regard to linguistic utterances. Usually, competent speakers are able to explicate the grammatical rules of the natural language in which they form and understand sentences only incompletely, if at all. Nonetheless, every adequately socialized speaker has at his disposal a know-how that enables him to distinguish phonetic utterances from mere sounds, to distinguish semantically meaningful and syntactically well-formed sentences from those that are deviant, and to order such sentences according to the degree of their deviation. This intuitively available knowledge of rules that competently speaking and acting subjects have, which can also be discursively articulated at any time, provides the required experiential basis for theories of action. Strictly behaviorist theories, on the other hand, depend exclusively on observational data. This fact gives rise to an important difference between the structures of the two types of theory and their relation to their respective object domain.

Theories that are to explain the phenomena accessible through the understanding of meaning [*Sinnverstehen*]—that is, the utterances and expressions of subjects capable of speech and action—must take the form of a systematic explication of the knowledge of rules based on which competent speakers and actors generate their expressions. Theory formation serves to reconstruct the systems of rules according to which meaningfully structured formations, sentences and actions, are produced. These generative rules need not be directly read off the surface structure of expressions. As with grammar, there may be deep structures, which underlie the surface structures that have been produced and yet are part of a competent speaker's implicit know-how; hence they are nonetheless known. The goal of such a theory is the hypothetical reconstruction of rule systems that disclose the internal logic of the rule-governed generation of intelligible surface structures. Let us now assume that these intelligible surface structures correspond to the empirical regularities of observable events (and behavioral responses). In this case we could compare the reconstruction of the abstract systems of rules underlying surface structures with theories of the empirical sciences from which we derive laws of nature that somehow "underlie" empirical regularities. But this comparison clearly reveals the difference in status of the two types of theories. The hypothetical reconstructions advance an almost essentialist claim that is absent from the nomological theories in the empirical sciences. For, insofar as the latter refer to the object domain of physically measurable events, the primitive terms of systems of nomological statements are primarily introduced by convention. They provide the idiom for a theoretical construct that can be corroborated indirectly through the derivation of lawlike hypotheses that are subject to confirmation. One might say that nomological hypotheses, if they are true, correspond to structures of a reality objectified in terms of physics or the behavioral sciences (or that they pick out invariant features of this objectified reality). But they cannot be said merely to reconstruct an intuitive knowledge that competent observers of this reality always already possess. Rather, the sort of knowledge thus produced is, as a rule, quite counterintuitive.

In contrast, the rational reconstructions of the knowledge of subjects capable of speech and action do raise such an essentialist claim. The primitive terms to be employed in the reconstruction of structures of operationally effective generative rules, therefore, are not introduced conventionally. Instead they are introduced in connection with categories that must be derivable from the self-understanding of the very subjects who produce these structures. As I see it, the essentialist moment consists in the fact that hypothetical reconstructions, if true, correspond not to structures of an objectified reality but to structures of the implicit know-how of competent subjects capable of judgment. What is to be explicated by these reconstructions are the operationally effective rules themselves.

I have discussed the metatheoretical decision whether meaning should be admitted as a primitive term in the social sciences by looking at three methodological implications of great import. Having done so, I can provide a provisional demarcation between objectivist and subjectivist approaches to theory formation. I shall call a theoretical program *subjectivist* if it conceives of society as a meaningfully structured system of life [*Lebenszusammenhang*], and as a system of symbolic expressions and structures that is continuously produced according to underlying abstract rules. Thus theory is given the task of reconstructing a process whereby a meaningfully structured social reality is produced. In contrast, I shall call a theoretical program *objectivist* if it conceives the life process of society not internally as a process of construction, that is, of the production of meaningful structures, but externally as a natural process that, like other processes, can be observed in its empirical regularities and explained by means of nomological hypotheses. In this sense, all strictly behaviorist theories, such as classical learning theory, are objectivist. At this point I prefer not to decide between these two competing approaches. I shall content myself with pointing out that the objectivist theoretical program, which has been quite successful within its limits, has to deal with difficulties arising from its methodological neglect of the symbolic prestructuring of social reality. These difficulties show up at the level of the measurement problems involved in attempting to reduce action to behavior, which have been discussed by Cicourel (1965) and others.[6] These difficulties are exemplified by what can now be considered the failed attempt to develop a behaviorist theory of language.[7] I do not want to enter into this discussion here. Instead I will limit myself in these lectures to the theoretical program of subjectivism. The generative theories of society [*Erzeugungstheorien*], as I shall call them from now on, have complementary difficulties to deal with. A theoretical program of this kind must answer three questions. Assuming that society is conceived as a process of generating a meaningfully structured reality:

(a) Who is the subject of this generative process, or is there no such subject?

(b) How is the mode of this generative process to be conceptualized—as cognitive activity (Kant and Hegel), as linguistic expression (Humboldt), as labor (Marx), as artistic creation (Schelling, Nietzsche), or as instinct (Freud)?

(c) And, finally: Are the underlying systems of rules according to which social reality is constructed invariant for all social systems, or do even these abstract rule systems develop historically, and is there possibly an inner logic of their development that can be reconstructed as well?

Before setting up a typology of how the most important generative theories of society have answered these questions, I want to discuss very briefly two further fundamental decisions concerning conceptual strategy that have great bearing for theory formation in the social sciences.

The *second metatheoretical decision* is whether intentional action is to be conceptualized in the form of purposive-rational action or in the form of communicative action. Let me first characterize these two types of action with reference to the status of the rules that govern behavior in each case. By *purposive-rational action* I understand either instrumental action or rational choice or a combination of the two. Instrumental action follows technical rules based on empirical knowledge. These rules imply conditional predictions regarding observable events, whether physical or social. Thus such predictions can prove to be correct or incorrect. Rational choice is governed by strategies based on analytical knowledge. They imply derivations from preference rules (value systems) and decision procedures. These propositions are derived either correctly or incorrectly. Purposive-rational action attains definite goals under given conditions. But whereas the means organized by instrumental action are appropriate or inappropriate according to criteria of effective control of reality, strategic action depends only on the correct assessment of possible behavioral options, which results from derivation using values and maxims alone.

By *communicative action* I understand symbolically mediated interaction. It is governed by binding norms that define reciprocal expectations about behavior and that must be understood and acknowledged or recognized by at least two acting subjects. Social norms are enforced through sanctions. Their meaning is objectified in symbolic expressions and is accessible only through ordinary language communication. Whereas the effectiveness of technical rules and strategies depends on the validity [*Gültigkeit*] of empirically true or analytically correct propositions, the validity [*Geltung*] of social norms is ensured by an intersubjective recognition that is based on a consensus about values or on mutual understanding. Violating a rule has different consequences in each case. Incompetent behavior, which violates proven technical rules or correct strategies, is condemned per se to failure through its lack of success. The "punishment," so to speak, is built into its foundering on the shoals of reality. Deviant behavior, on the other hand, which violates prevailing norms, triggers sanctions that are connected with the rules only externally, by convention. Learned rules of purposive-rational action provide us with a regime of skills; in contrast, internalized norms furnish us with a regime of personality structures. Skills enable us to solve problems, whereas motivations allow us to conform to norms. Table 1 summarizes these definitions. They require a more precise analysis, which I cannot undertake here.

Theory formation in the social sciences has the option of defining the object domain to comprise either actions of the strategic type only or both strategic and communicative actions. Strategic action can be considered as a limiting case of communicative action; it oc-

Table 1
Rules of Action

	Social Norms	Technical and Strategic Rules
Linguistic Means of Definition	intersubjectively shared ordinary language	context-free language
Elements of Definition	reciprocal normative expectations of behavior	conditional predictions; conditional imperatives
Mechanisms of Acquisition	internalization of roles	learning of skills and qualifications
Function of the Type of Action	maintenance of institutions (conformity to norms based on reciprocal reinforcement)	problem-solving (goal attainment, defined in terms of means-ends relations)
Sanctions for Violating Rules	punishment based on conventional sanctions; failure against social authority	lack of success; failure against reality

curs when ordinary language communication between interlocutors breaks down as a means of maintaining consensus, and each assumes an objectifying attitude toward the other. For strategic action is based on rules for the purposive-rational choice of means; and, in principle, each actor can make this choice by herself. Maxims of behavior in strategic action are determined by the interests of maximizing gains and minimizing losses in the context of competition. In this case, my other is no longer an alter ego whose expectations I can fulfill (or disappoint) according to intersubjectively recognized norms. Rather, she is an opponent whose decisions I seek to influence indirectly by means of punishments and rewards. Instrumental actions, on the other hand, are not social actions at all; rather, they can appear as components of social actions (i.e., as elements of role definitions). If only strategic actions are admitted, we can develop rational choice theories such as theories of exchange. If communicative actions are admitted as well, we can develop conventional theories of action such as those of Weber or Parsons.

The *third metatheoretical decision* that I consider to be of major consequence is whether we should choose an atomistic or a so-called holistic approach. I cannot go into the details of the extensive literature on this issue.[8] Both conceptual strategies seem to me to be feasible, although the different theories have different domains of application and capacities. At the level of theories of action, the atomistic approach takes the form of methodological individualism. J. W. N. Watkins (in agreement with Popper) has formulated two independent postulates: (a) "the ultimate constituents of the social world are individual people who act more or less appropriately in the light of their dispositions and the understanding of their situation."[9] Thus all social phenomena must be analyzable in the form of statements about the actions of individual subjects. Statements in a theoretical idiom, which contains expressions for supraindividual social entities, such as roles, institutions, value systems, and traditions, are inadmissible unless they can be reduced to statements in another theoretical idiom in which the only predicates are for acting subjects, their utterances, and their motivations. The second postulate is that (b) "no social tendency exists which could not be altered if the individuals concerned both wanted to alter it and possessed the appropriate information."[10] This stronger claim has the status of a philosophical assumption. It states that subjects capable of speech and action are the only agents of change in the historical development of social systems. Social change can be explained with reference to the properties of supraindividual units (such as systems, groups, or structures) if and only if these supraindividual properties are reducible to properties of individual subjects capable of speech and action. The counterposition to an individualistic theory of action is represented today by social systems theory (such as the work of Deutsch, Parsons, and Luhmann). Systems theory takes into account the fact that the structure of social norms transcends the subjectively intended meaning of individuals acting according to norms. Systems are introduced as units that can solve objectively given problems through learning processes that transcend individual subjects.

The three options that I have mentioned, from which a conceptual strategy for the social sciences must be chosen, offer convenient criteria for classifying the most important theoretical approaches, as indicated in table 2.

I do not want to examine the relative fruitfulness of these various theoretical approaches. This overview is intended rather for the

Table 2
Approaches to Social Theory

Primitive Terms of a Theory of Action / Theoretical Approach	Meaning as primitive term		
	not admissible	admissible	
	behavior	strategic action	communicative (and strategic) action
atomistic	behaviorist psychology	rational choice theories (e.g., pure economics)	"interpretive" sociology (e.g., ethnomethodology)
holistic	biological systems theory	social cybernetics (e.g., organizational sociology)	structuralist and functionalist systems theories; symbolic interactionism

purpose of classifying the generative theories of society that I am interested in. Obviously they do not belong among strictly behaviorist theories; no more, however, do they belong among theories of strategic action. These theories incorporate assumptions of rationality that obtain—approximately—but for limited segments of social reality. Both rational choice theories and social cybernetic models have a normative analytical status. They can be applied only on one of two presuppositions. The first is that subjects act rationally and that the assumed maxims of behavior are in fact the basis of their actions. The second is that the self-regulating systems are stabilized in precisely the state that is conventionally postulated to be optimal. Generative theories of society cannot belong to this type of theory, since they claim to comprehend the life process of society as a whole and, in particular, as a concrete process of the generation of meaning structures. They do not content themselves with segments of reality that can be seen as approximating models of rationality. In other words, they are not satisfied with a normative analytical status. Therefore they must be classified under the type of theory that appears in the right hand column of the table.

To be able to use this framework to differentiate between different construction theories of society, we must return to the questions that already forced themselves upon us with regard to the as yet unclear concept of the generation of meaningfully organized structures of life. If I am right, we can try to clarify the generative process of society by means of the following four models.

The *first model* is that of the knowing or "judging" subject. Kant examined the necessary subjective conditions of the possibility of empirical knowledge in general and, in so doing, introduced the concept of the constitution of the objects of experience. Following this pattern, Husserl conceived the constitution of the everyday world of lived experience (lifeworld) in which we can have experiences, relate to objects and persons, and perform actions. Alfred Schütz in turn derived a constitutive theory of society from Husserl's analysis. The epistemological origins of this phenomenological theory of society are evident in the title of the well-known study by Schütz's students Berger and Luckmann.[11] They speak of the social construction of reality. They conceive of the generative process of society as producing an image of reality in relation to which subjects orient their behavior toward one another. That is why for Berger and Luckmann sociology and the sociology of knowledge are basically identical. For the constitution of social reality coincides with the generation of a worldview that orients social action. Constitutive theories attribute the process of generation to an acting subject. This subject can be either an intelligible ego modeled after the empirical individual subject or, as in Hegel and Marx and dialectical social theory, a species-subject constituting itself in history. Later we shall see that precisely these concepts of a generalized individual ("transcendental") consciousness or of a collective consciousness create specific difficulties for transferring the constitutive model from the world of possible experience to society.

The *second and third models* of the generative process of society are subjectless rule systems. I have in mind structuralist social anthropology on the one hand and sociological systems theory on the other. Both structuralism and systems theory conceive of society as a system of either symbolic forms or information channels produced by underlying structures. In both cases the deep structures are without a subject. They are anonymous systems of rules. Structuralism models these on grammar, whereas systems theory thinks of them as self-regulating. The former is based on structural linguistics going back to Saussure, the latter on cybernetics, which has been transposed to apply to organisms. The basic structures are subjectless in the same sense as is the grammar of a natural language or a self-regulating machine. What first appears to be an advantage turns out to be a weakness specific to this point of view: The constitutive model no more shows the way out of the monadic shell of the active subject than the systems model can incorporate speaking and acting subjects and, especially, their interrelations. For the system of grammatical rules requires competent speakers for its actualization, whereas the machine regulates itself and has no need of any subject at all. In neither case is the paradigm suited for giving an accurate account of how intersubjectively binding meaning structures are generated.

For such an account, we can resort to the *fourth model*, that of ordinary language communication (speech and interaction). Here we are dealing with the generation of interpersonal situations of speaking and acting together—that is, with the form of the intersubjectivity of possible understanding [*Verständigung*]. The underlying abstract systems of rules must be conceived in such a way as to explain two things. The first is the pragmatic generation of the common basis of intersubjectively shared meaning. The second is the more specifically linguistic generation of sentences that we use in speech acts for purposes of both cognition and action. This model permits incorporating the relation of intersubjectivity as one of the main topics of a generative theory of society. Examples are G. H. Mead's social psychology of role-taking and the later Wittgenstein's theory of language games. The generative rules underlying role-taking and language games are conceived as subjectless, just like the grammatical rules of a natural language. However, they are constructed in such a way that the surface structures to which they give rise include not only symbolic forms such as sentences and actions, but also the subjects of speech and action themselves, who are formed through ordinary language communication. Mead's social psychology is at the same time a theory of socialization. The meaningful structures that a generative theory of society must account for comprise both personality structures and the forms of intersubjectivity within which subjects express themselves by means of speech and interaction.

Generative theories of society that in one way or another presuppose a transcendental subject I shall from now on refer to as *constitutive theories of society*, those that base the generative process on structures lacking a subject *system theories*, and, finally, those that accept abstract systems of rules for generating intersubjective relations in which subjects themselves are formed, *communicative theories of society*. We can add, as a differentiating feature, that some theories allow for the historical development of the active subject or underlying rule systems, whereas others either keep to a strict dichotomy between transcendental achievements and constituted phenomena or at least exclude the logical reconstruction of the history of the constitutive factors. This yields the classification shown in table 3.

The informational content of this rough overview is to be found in the—naturally empty—bottom right-hand corner. The table serves to delimit a theoretical approach that has not yet been adequately developed. Therefore I cannot refer to an existing body of work. On the other hand, I can at least draw on Mead's theory of role-taking and Wittgenstein's theory of language games. For they prefigure the universal pragmatics that I take to be the right kind of foundation for social theory and whose basic tenets I should like to develop. But I would first like to consider the example of a constitutive theory of society that derives from Kant. This example will allow us to be clear from the outset about the premises to which we are committed as soon as we try to conceive of the learning process of society as a generative process. Moreover, the characteristic weakness of constitutive theories will come to light precisely in the problem with which communicative theory begins: the derivation of intersubjective relations from the monological framework of transcendental philosophy of consciousness.

Georg Simmel devoted a well-known appendix to the first chapter of his major work to the question: "How is society possible?"[12] This is the analogue to the basic question of the *Critique of Pure Reason:* How is knowledge of nature possible? Kant had sought to answer this question by demonstrating that the knowing subject itself constitutes

Objectivist and Subjectivist Approaches to Theory Formation

Table 3
Generative Theories of Society

Types historical development of constitutive factors	Constitutive Theories *Generative theories of society*		Systems Theories	Communicative Theories
	atomistic	holistic	holistic	holistic
not admissible	Neo-Kantianism (Rickert, Adler); Phenomenology (Husserl, Schütz)	romantic social theories (O. Spann)	structuralism (Lévy-Strauss)	symbolic interactionism (G. H. Mead); theory of language games (Wittgenstein, Winch)
admissible	Marxist phenomenology (Marcuse, Sartre, Kosik)	dialectical social theory (Lukács, Adorno)	systems theory of societal development (Parsons, Luhmann)	?

nature as the realm of the objects of possible experience. He analyzed the necessary subjective conditions of intuition and judgment that are the a priori conditions of the possibility of experience, that is, the organization of the manifold of sensations as phenomena in a totality of lawlike connections. In Simmel we find a classic formulation of the attempt to extend this approach of a constitutive theory of the knowledge of nature to a constitutive theory of society: not of the knowledge of society, but of society itself.

It is very tempting to treat as an analogous matter [analogous to the question of the a priori conditions of the knowledge of nature—J. H.] the question of the aprioristic conditions under which society is possible. Here, also, we find individual elements. In a certain sense, they too, like sense perceptions, stay forever isolated from one another. They, likewise, are synthesized into the unity of society only by means of a conscious process which correlates the individual existence of the single element with that of the other, and which does so only in certain forms and according to certain rules.[13]

However, Simmel immediately notes the key difference. From the perspective of a constitutive theory, nature and society are not at the same level of analysis. "Nature" can be defined as an object domain of knowledge only in relation to the synthetic activity of the knowing subject, who creates unity in the manifold of intuition. But the knowing subject encounters society as an already constituted unity—one constituted by empirical subjects themselves. The question of how nature is constituted refers to the problem of the *knowledge* of nature; that of how society is constituted refers to the problem of how society is possible. The process of social life occurs on the level of constitutive activities and not, like the process of natural events, at the level of what is already constituted. In other words, the processes of consciousness whereby societal subjects constitute society take place at the same transcendental level at which the knowing subject constitutes nature as the object of possible experience. Thus the sphere of society attains a type of objectivity in relation to the knowing mind that nature cannot claim in relation to the subject involved in knowing nature.

[T]here is a decisive difference between the unity of a society and the unity of nature. It is this: In the Kantian view (which we follow here), the unity of nature emerges in the observing subject exclusively; it is produced exclusively by him in the sense data, and on the basis of sense data, which are in themselves heterogeneous. By contrast, the unity of society needs no observer. It is directly realized by its own elements because these elements are themselves conscious and synthesizing units. . . . Societal unification needs no factors outside its own component elements. Each of them exercises the function which the psychic energy of the observer exercises in regard to external nature: the consciousness of constituting a unity with the others is actually all there is to this unity.[14]

Simmel goes on to say that

Owing to these circumstances, the question of how society is possible implies a methodology which is wholly different from that for the question of how nature is possible. The latter question is answered by the forms of cognition, whereby the subject synthesizes the given elements into "nature." By contrast, the former is answered by the conditions which reside a priori in the elements themselves, whereby they combine, in reality, into the synthesis "society."[15]

This consideration is of central importance for the starting point of all generative theories of society, regardless of whether they follow

Dilthey, Rickert, Husserl, or Wittgenstein or are based directly on Kant or Hegel and Marx. For it is the foundation of a dualistic philosophy of science, which on principle methodologically sets off the cultural or social sciences and humanities from the natural sciences. Nature is regarded as an object domain that can be accounted for in terms of the constitutive activities of the knowing subject. In contrast, the construction of society by means of the synthetic activities of societal subjects produces something that is singularly objective in comparison to nature. It confronts the knowing subject as a unity that is already meaningfully structured, leaving the subject with the possibility only of reconstructing or reproducing a constitutive act that has already been accomplished. This dualism has three implications for the theoretical program of the social sciences, all of which can already be found in Simmel.

First, a constitutive social theory goes beyond the sphere of cognition of nature, that is, of science. The preconstituted world that social science must reconstruct in order to be able to explain societal processes is the sphere of prescientific experience and of everyday practices. That is why the analysis of the lifeworld becomes the focus of Husserl's phenomenology.

Second, transcendental analysis, when applied to the noncognitive, practical accomplishments of a subjectivity that is no longer understood merely as the subject of possible knowledge, leads to conceiving of the system of social life as a "fact of knowledge," to use Simmel's expression. The program of examining the necessary subjective conditions of possible sociation with means borrowed from epistemology is by no means self-evident. For

the phenomenon which arises from these processes of sociation and which receives its norms from their forms is not cognition but consists of practical processes and actual situations. Nevertheless, what is to be examined (as the general idea of sociation) in regard to its conditions is something cognitive, namely, the consciousness of sociating·or of being sociated. This consciousness is perhaps better called knowledge (*Wissen*) than cognition (*Erkenntnis*). For here, the subject is not confronting an object of which it gradually acquires a theoretical picture. . . . It is the processes of interaction which signify to the individual the fact of being sociated—not an abstract fact, to be sure, but a fact capable of abstract expression. What are the forms that must underlie this fact? What specific categories are there that human beings must come with, so to speak, so that this consciousness may arise? And what, therefore, are the forms that this consciousness—society as a fact of knowledge—has to support? These questions may be called (the subject matter of) the epistemology of society.[16]

This turn in the argument has a noteworthy implication. If the system of social life is constructed out of cognitive acts, then it rests on the *facticity* of the same *validity claims* as are posited with every form of knowledge. Consciousness, we say, can be true or false, correct or incorrect, rational or irrational. Therefore a society that is meaningfully structured by synthetic acts of consciousness and is constituted as a "fact of knowledge" has an immanent relation to truth. I shall elaborate on this later. Again it was Husserl who first said this and developed a theory of truth that incorporated everyday practice.

Third, Simmel had already discovered the difficulty with which all constitutive theories of society struggle in vain. Epistemology is concerned with the relation between the transcendental (or individual) subject and its cognitive object, and this relation is in principle monological. Society, in contrast, is constituted through the synthetic accomplishments of a multiplicity of subjects, who mutually recognize one another as subjects. But how can the construction of this intersubjectivity be conceptualized by means of an epistemology that is committed to a monological approach? The Other is encountered as a center of possible constitutive accomplishments on the same level as the knowing ego:

[T]he other mind has for me the same reality which I have myself, and this reality is very different from that of a material object. . . . This for-itself (*Für-sich*) of the other does not prevent us from turning it into our representation. In other words, something which can by no means be resolved into our representing, nevertheless becomes its content, and thus the product of our representative capacity. This phenomenon is the fundamental psychologico-epistemological paradigm and problem of sociation.[17]

This problem was taken up by Husserl, who dealt with it most subtly in his *Cartesian Meditations*.[18]

The Phenomenological Constitutive Theory of Society: The Fundamental Role of Claims to Validity and the Monadological Foundations of Intersubjectivity

It is no accident that the most influential constitutive social theory in contemporary sociology, especially in the United States, is based on the work of Husserl. For Husserl's phenomenology is better suited than Kant's transcendental philosophy to expanding the constitutive theory of knowledge into a theory of society. There are two reasons for this. First, Husserl differs from Kant through his recourse to the lifeworld as the level in which the theory of knowledge is grounded. Second, he uses the concept of constitution in a descriptive manner. I should like to discuss these two points before going into the two problems that must be solved by any constitutive social theory, including those that have overcome the limitations of a philosophy of consciousness: the problem of society's immanent relation to truth, and the problem of the foundation of intersubjectivity.

(a) Like Husserl, Kant analyzed the constitution of a world of possible experience. Yet unlike Husserl, he focused on objectivity, that is, on the necessary subjective conditions of possible knowledge of nature. For Kant believed that accounting for the validity of the most exact empirical judgments (that is, the theoretical propositions of contemporary physics) would at the same time account for the transcendental bases of experience in general. Husserl challenges the self-evidence of this view in his famous treatise, *The Crisis of the European Sciences.*[1] He conceives the object domain of the natural sciences not as the infrastructure of the objects of possible experience in general, but as a derived artificial product. This artifice can be adequately accounted for only if we disclose the everyday lifeworld as the forgotten foundation of meaning. Since Galileo, the natural sciences have dealt with a form of "nature" that has emerged from a transformation of prescientific everyday experience, organized as a lifeworld, rather than from a synthesis of the manifold of sensations given prior to any organized experience. This commonsense experience of daily life is at first relative to the body and its organs: The perceptual field is kinesthetically structured. It is tailored to the perspective of an ego: The experience of space and time is centered in a subject. Second, everyday experience is formed not only in accordance with cognitive ends but in connection with affective attitudes, intentions, and practical interventions in the objective world. Needs and emotional attitudes, as well as valuations and actions, form a horizon of natural interests; and only in this context can experiences come into being and be corrected. Third, everyday experience is not a private matter. It is part of an intersubjectively shared world in which I live, speak, and act together with other subjects. Intersubjectively communalized experience is expressed in symbolic systems, especially natural language, in which accumulated knowledge is pregiven to the individual subject as cultural tradition. At this level we encounter cultural objects, which are expressions of the life of subjects capable of action and speech. The sciences, too, are such cultural objects.

Husserl makes us realize that Kant naively took as his starting point the object domain of physics and failed to see that scientific theories of this type are produced in a community of investigators (Peirce). This community, in turn, must take for granted the factual validity of its everyday lifeworld:

Since this is to be a matter of spiritual functions which exercise their accomplishment in all experiencing and thinking, indeed in each and every preoccupation of the human world-life, functions through which the world of experience, as the constant horizon of existing things, has any meaning and validity for us, it would certainly be understandable that all objective sciences would lack the precise knowledge of what is most fundamental, namely, the knowledge of what could procure meaning and validity for the theoretical structures of objective knowledge with any meaning and validity and thus first gives them the dignity of a knowledge which is ultimately grounded.[2]

Thus we misconstrue the constitution of the world of possible experience if we choose the object domain of scientific knowledge as our paradigm and fail to see that science is anchored in the lifeworld and that this lifeworld is the basis of the meaning of scientifically objectified reality. The constitutive theory of empirical knowledge must therefore *presuppose* a constitutive theory of the lifeworld. The latter, in turn, comprises a constitutive theory of society (as part of a so-called ontology of the lifeworld[3]).

(b) But this is not the only reason why phenomenology is congenial to the project of a constitutive theory of society. Husserl gives the concept of constitution itself a descriptive turn, so that an interpretive sociology based on understanding [*Verstehen*], such as that developed by Alfred Schütz, can consistently incorporate Husserl's analyses of the constitution of the lifeworld. Here again, Husserl differs from Kant. Kant conceives the constitution of the objects of possible experience as the genesis of the necessary subjective conditions of the synthesis of a manifold. Thus he arrives at a general theory of the activities and underlying structures of the knowing mind. By contrast, Husserl from the outset directs the meditating phenomenologist's reflective gaze at the way in which sensory and categorial objects are "given" to him. Unlike Kant, Husserl does not want to reconstruct the one universal mode of objectification through which the experience of reality becomes at all possible. Rather, he wants to grasp descriptively the varying modes of the "self-givenness" of objects. For any object whatever that remains the same throughout our changing modes of consciousness, we can "see," as it were, how its meaning and being are shaped in how it is given to us by our synthetic accomplishments. True, Husserl, too, assumes a universally productive subjectivity. But this subjectivity generates an *open* horizon of possible objects, which allows a manifold of various types of objectivity that can be grasped only descriptively.[4] In this way, Husserl clears the way for a constitutive theory of society, which adopts a descriptive attitude and studies the universal structures of the lifeworld. A sociology that proceeds phenomenologically understands the social lifeworld from the outset as a world constituted by synthetic accomplishments. In the most general structure of these activities it recognizes the typical meaning structures that intersubjectively communalized subjects must continually produce insofar as they at all orient themselves to objects of possible experience in their everyday practice.

Husserl's phenomenology has one final advantage over Kant's as a contribution to a sociological version of constitutive theory. Phenomenological investigation takes as its frame of reference not an anonymous consciousness in general, but rather the individual transcendental ego of the phenomenological observer (who practices the *epochē*). Husserl assumes a multiplicity of transcendental egos who constitute the social lifeworld in relation to one another despite the cognitive priority of each one's own subjectivity. By contrast, Kant (at least in his theoretical philosophy) strictly distinguishes between a plurality of empirical egos and a singular transcendental consciousness in general. Thus the problem of the possible transcendental community of subjects who first monadically produce their world cannot even arise for him.[5]

I now want to examine more closely two problems that result from the phenomenological foundation of a constitutive theory of society. We shall see that these problems arise for any conceivable generative theory of society. I want to show that they cannot be solved within the framework of a theory of consciousness and that they necessitate the transition to a theory of linguistic communication.

Every society that we conceive of as a meaningfully structured system of life has an immanent relation to truth. For the reality of meaning structures is based on the peculiar facticity of claims to validity: In general, these claims are naively accepted—that is, they are presumed to be fulfilled. But validity claims can, of course, be called into question. They raise a claim to legitimacy, and this legitimacy can be problematized: It can be confirmed or rejected. We can speak of "truth" here only in the broad sense of the legitimacy of a claim that can be fulfilled or disappointed. Thus we say, for example, that an opinion or assertion, as well as a hope, wish, or guess, is correct or justified, that a promise or announcement has been properly made, that advice has been honorably given, that a measure has been properly taken, a description or an evaluation correctly done. In everyday interactions, we rely naively on an unsurveyable wealth of such claims to legitimacy. It is always only individual claims that emerge from this background and that are thematized and checked in case of disappointment.

Husserl captures the specific character of factually operative meaning structures with the concept of intentionality, which he derives primarily from Brentano. Intentional experiences have the character of being the consciousness *of something*. They are directed toward something in the way that an opinion, expectation, or wish is paradigmatically oriented toward an object or state of affairs. Sentences formed with intentional expressions, such as "believe," "expect," and "wish," always require a direct object or objective clause of the form "I hate (insult) x" or "I mean that p." This grammatical form expresses what Husserl wanted to grasp immediately at the level of consciousness with the concept of intentionality. What distinguishes intentional experiences from one another is the meaning with which different acts of consciousness are directed toward their objects. Different intentions may be directed at the same object, in which case they have, as Husserl says (in the first *Logical Investigation*), the same real [*reell*] content but different intentional contents. The latter he also refers to as the intentional object (or *noema*, as he calls it from *Ideas* onward). It is to Husserl's credit that he elucidated the remarkable intentional structure of our consciousness and demonstrated the immanent truth relation of intentional experiences.[6]

We intend an object that is not present to us, but which we know could be directly given to us. Intentionality requires the possibility of the virtual presence of objects that could also be actually present. Otherwise we would not be able to take quite different intentional attitudes toward the same object. The intentional structure of our consciousness requires the possibility of a difference between the merely mediated and the immediate givenness of objects. At the linguistic level, we can illustrate this difference in terms of the division of the declarative sentence into a subject expression and a predicate expression. The subject expression, a noun or definite description, refers to a particular object that can be determined by the positive or negative ascription of predicates. This reference does not require that the object denoted be present. Rather, it suffices that the object can be represented at all as an identifiable object. It is to this feature of the logic of language that we owe the possibility of context-independent language use. Indeed, the most notable achievement of linguistic communication is precisely the representation of objects and states of affairs that are absent.

Within the bounds of a theory of consciousness, however, Husserl cannot make the distinction between context-dependent experience and context-transcendent representation by means of referential expressions (which refer to the context or situation). Instead, he interprets the difference between the mediated and immediate givenness of objects as a difference between nonintuitive givenness and intuitively fulfilled givenness. The meaning of an intentional object then always requires the possibility of the intuitively immediate presence of the object. The intuitive richness of an object that is given in evidence can hence be understood as the fulfillment of a corresponding intention of the object. Ideally, the stages of fulfillment point to a goal in which the entire intention has been fulfilled. The full intuitive presence of the object leaves, so to speak, no trace of unfulfilled intention. This conception is connected with a concept of truth as evidence, discussion of which I shall postpone for the moment. Husserl introduces his theory of truth without further justification. He considers it simply "the principle of all principles: that . . . everything originarily offered to us in 'intuition' is to be accepted simply as what it is presented as being."[7] Truth can then be defined with reference to the concept of intention. Truth is the identifying thought, accompanied by an evidential experience, of something intended, as coinciding with a corresponding intuitively given object. Conversely, it follows from this that all intentional experiences are immanently and necessarily related to truth.

What matters for my present purposes is the following consideration. Every intention is usually connected with a "positing," whereby the act of consciousness goes beyond the intended object and anticipates its factual givennness. The quality of positing consists in anticipating the intuitive fulfillment of the intention. The unfulfilled act posits the intentional object as existing. In so doing, it associates with it the claim that if the object were to come to the stage of self-givenness, it would appear just as it is intended, and not otherwise. Such a claim is either legitimate or illegitimate; its legitimacy can be demonstrated only by the intuitive fulfillment of the originally "empty" intention. Of course, positing qualities can also be bracketed or "neutralized," in which case we set aside the question of the legitimacy of the claim that a given intention can be fulfilled precisely as anticipated. Intentions that are not neutralized in this sense, however, are connected with a validity claim that can be undermined at any time by a failed attempt to bring the intended object to adequate self-givenness.

The lifeworld as a whole is also posited. For the meaning structures that constitute the lifeworld exist only in the manifold of validity claims inherent in them. These claims come together in the "general thesis of the natural attitude," that is, in the basic belief of naive realism that "the" world in which I find myself exists and has always existed as an actuality that surrounds me.[8] The general thesis encompasses the totality of life in the natural world.

There we move in a current of ever new experiences, judgments, valuations, and decisions. In each of these acts, the ego is directed toward objects in its surrounding world, dealing with them in one way or another. It is of them that we are conscious in these acts themselves, sometimes simply as actual, sometimes in modalities of actuality (for example as possible, doubtful, etc.). None of these acts, and none of the validities contained in them, is isolated. In their intentions they necessarily imply an infinite horizon of inactive [inaktuelle] validity which simultaneously function with them in flowing mobility.[9]

Interestingly enough, Husserl extends the positing characteristics that he derived from a particular class of intentions to all classes of intentions. At first, positings are connected with so-called doxic acts that are oriented to matters of fact. For the belief that an intended object in fact does or does not exist as intended is associated with such intentions as perceptions, representations, memories, judgments, and so on. Moreover, it would appear that only acts of this sort imply the kind of modalities of Being—that is, modifications of the absolute certainty of the existence of an object (of *Urdoxa*)—such that I consider it possible or probable or doubtful that an intended object will appear in reality just as it is intended. But if only doxic acts were capable of truth, then Husserl could not support the assertion that positings are connected with *all* intentions. Indeed, he would have to abandon the concept of intention itself: For this concept always contains the anticipation of possible fulfillment through evident self-givenness, as well as, in principle, the possible disappointment of such fulfillment; and it thus always has an immanent relation to truth. This would also render untenable the extremely strong thesis that the lifeworld itself is based on the facticity of accepted validity claims that in principle can nonetheless be problematized. If, on the other hand, *all* intentional experiences have an immanent relation to truth, that is, if all intentions are defined by the possibility of their intuitive fulfillment (or disappointment), then acts of the "sphere of emotion and will," as Husserl calls them, must also imply positings. There are two arguments for this.

First, all emotional and volitional acts, such as fears and desires, and decisions and expressions of will, are built upon acts in which an object is intended. Intentional statements such as "I fear (or hope or desire) that this man will depart" refer to a state of affairs that may or may not obtain. (In our examples, the same state of affairs is represented in each case by the propositional content "that this man will depart.") Therefore emotive and volitional acts imply, as Husserl says, potential positings: They are potentially thetic. Second, however, emotive and volitional acts also contain positings in themselves, and not only with regard to the potentially existing states of affairs to which they refer. The types of positings for emotive and volitional acts are grounded. Husserl assumes specific positings that can be explicated as value judgments, such as that an intended object *is* or *is not* actually (or probably or presumably) pleasing or repulsive, lovely or horrible, desirable or indifferent, beautiful or ugly, good or evil: "Even in valuing, wishing, willing, something is 'posited,' apart from the doxic positionality 'inherent' in them."[10] And elsewhere:

On the one hand, there are new characteristics which are *analogous to the modes of belief* but possess, at the same time, *themselves* doxo-logical positableness; on the other hand, connected with the novel moments there are also novel "*apprehensions*," and a new sense becomes constituted. . . . with it no new determining parts of mere "things" are constituted, but instead *values of things,* value-qualities, or concrete Objects with values: beauty and ugliness, goodness and badness; the use-Object, the art work, the machine, the book, the action, the deed, and so forth.[11]

Even nondoxically performed acts of consciousness, therefore, imply claims to validity that can be naively presupposed or problematized, accepted or rejected.

The universal application of the concept of intuitively fulfillable intention guarantees that *all* meaningfully structured formations are capable of truth, whether they have cognitive meaning or primarily emotional and volitional meaning. That is why Husserl can adopt Cartesian language. He calls all intentional objects *cogitata,* regardless of whether they are associated with doxic or nondoxic positing qualities. Thus the constitution of everyday lived practices can be conceived according to principles of a constitutive theory of knowledge under the headings *ego, cogitatio,* and *cogitatum.* The entire life process must be reducible to the performance of acts by a productive subjectivity, which articulates itself in meaning structures of possible objects of intuitive experience.

From the fact that intentional life universally is oriented to truth, Husserl drew an ethical conclusion. He inferred from it the remarkable demand for absolute self-responsibility on the part of sociated human beings. This radical notion is developed in his much neglected essay, "The Idea of Individual and Community Life in Absolute Self-Responsibility":[21]

Here clearly emerges the universality with which the realm of knowledge encompasses all types of activities that derive from emotional and volitional subjectivity. Correlatively, however, the sphere of the valuating emotions and the will, in their endeavors and activities, extends to the entirety of subjectivity and all its intentional functions. What this means for science, however, is that all of evaluative and practical reason is reflected and objectified in science as the objectification of cognitive reason. In other words, all truth, including every evaluative and practical truth, finds expression and is determined in the cognitive forms of theoretical truth, where it also takes on the forms of cognitive justification.[13]

Absolute self-responsibility is the subjective counterpart of the intentional structure of the lifeworld; for the positings of the lifeworld imply an interest in proving their presumptive legitimacy. On both the personal as well as the political level, a life is irresponsible if it contents itself with the facticity of claims to validity without attempting to verify the lifeworld's universal truth claim through the equally comprehensive exercise of philosophical reason. According to this idea, human practice could be said to be radically responsible only if the constituting activities from which the lifeworld is constructed were first reconstituted in the phenomenological attitude, and all empty positings were uncovered and all unfulfillable intentions rejected:

We must consider that every form of human action, willing, and feeling can become the object of sciences in which it becomes the theoretical object, and that every instance of theoretical knowledge can find immediate normative application, in which it becomes the rule for a possible practice, etc. Since it is the vocation of philosophy as universal science to be the original source from which all other sciences draw their ultimate justification, we can then understand that such a philosophy can be no theoretical fancy to human beings. Rather, a philosophical life must be understood as life itself based on absolute self-responsibility.[14]

For Husserl this contemplative life is not only the business of the individual philosopher but also a political program:

This question, how—ideally speaking—a majority if not the totality of persons who are in possible relations of mutual understanding or are already linked as a community through personal relations would lead a life for which they could take absolute responsibility, leads to another: is communal life of this sort conceivable without a community of wills directed at such a life based on absolute responsibility? Furthermore, is such a life possible if the idea of it has not first been worked out scientifically, epistemologically, that is, unless we have a normative science about it (ethics)?[15]

Thus far I have sought to explicate Husserl's own train of thought. The occasional references to the philosophy of language were for purposes of clarification only and not of critique. Now, however, I should like to point out certain difficulties that raise the question of whether an adequate treatment of the immanent truth relation of a meaningfully structured lifeworld does not rupture the framework of a theory of consciousness and demand instead to be approached through philosophy of language. Unlike Tugendhat, I shall not deal with the difficulties inherent in the phenomenological theory of meaning (which originates in Husserl's deriving the concept of the intentional object from the reification of the predicates we attribute to identifiable objects). Instead I should like to call attention to the difficulties entailed by the concept of truth as evidence.

We have seen that Husserl defines truth with reference to the intuitive fulfillment of an intention as the immediate presence of the intentional object (for which there is a corresponding experience of evidence). This requires an intuition sui generis for all categorial objects, which appear in every form of judgment. That is why Husserl develops his doctrine of categorial intuition, with which he attempts to render plausible the idea of a nonsensible intuition analogous to sensible intuition. The force of the conceptual strategy that leads Husserl to develop such a conception is understandable. But he provides no convincing argument that the concept of "categorial intuition" can be conceived of in any logically consistent manner at all or that the expression can be used nonmetaphorically. The problem is solved as soon as we regard what Husserl calls categorial objects, such as syntactic forms or mathematical relations, as symbolic constructs generated in accordance with rules, and refrain from imputing to them quasi-objects toward which intentions can be directed. For then a claim to validity can no longer be connected with an individual category; rather it applies to whether syntactic or mathematical forms, for instance, are generated in accordance with the rules.

Quite apart from this, it seems to me questionable whether Husserl correctly conceived the function of sensible intuition that provides the model for categorial intuition. The concept of the "self-givenness" of an object relies on the assumption that sense experience gives us intuitive access to something that is immediately and evidently given. This assumption is difficult to defend, as some of Husserl's own analyses indicate (see, for example, *Erfahrung und Urteil*). Every intuition, no matter how originary, includes categorial determinations; every perception, no matter how pre-predicative, contains hypothetical elements that go beyond anything that is actually given. The paradigmatic experience that may have been in Husserl's mind when he formulated his concept of truth as evidence can scarcely be found at the level of experiences of sensory evidence. It is more likely to be found at the level of experiences of construction. When we generate symbolic objects according to rules—

whether we are constructing a numerical series or geometrical figures, performing a composition for piano, or producing a sentence—an intention is always fulfilled by an object that is generated and was previously intended as such.[16]

However, *this* intuition of the success of a construction owes its ability to guarantee certainty precisely to the circumstance that we ourselves have produced the symbolic object according to underlying generative rules. Consequently we can understand the object perfectly, for the history of its genesis is transparent to us. The intuition of generative activity thus is not be confused with the intuition of what is immediately given, a concept that Husserl introduced programmatically by appealing to the model of sense experience.[17] Even perceptions depend on an interpretive framework. Therefore they contain hypothetical claims to validity, which can by no means be redeemed by recourse to elementary perceptions at some deeper level; for every sense experience can be problematized. If, however, there is no recourse to an ultimate, underlying foundation of intuitive self-givenness, and if, as Peirce convincingly demonstrated long ago, we must abandon the concept of truth as evidence, then the claims to validity implicit in intentional experiences cannot be redeemed intuitively, but only discursively. It is not intuitions but arguments that can lead us to acknowledge or reject the legitimacy of claims to validity that have been problematized.

Husserl's concept of intentionality stands and falls with the concept of truth as evidence. It was derived from the model of a solitary, monadic subject orienting itself to an object in meaning-giving acts. There is much to be said for reformulating this concept in linguistic terms. We shall then have to distinguish those intentions that signify simply that we understand the meaning of symbolic forms that have been produced and employed in conformity with rules from those intentions that involve a "positing," that is, a validity claim that extends beyond well-formedness or intelligibility. *These* intentions are paradigmatically connected with sentences that are uttered in situations where subjects capable of speech and action attempt to reach mutual understanding. In this version, Husserl's thesis of a truth claim immanent in a meaningfully structured lifeworld becomes interesting. We have seen that a communicative theory of society regards the surface structure of the lifeworld as a system of symbolic forms instead of as a stream of intentional experiences. But this theory, too, must acknowledge that the facticity of the validity claims implicit in these utterances is constitutive of the mode of being of the lifeworld. These positings are simultaneously based on experience and tradition and are culturally habitualized. But they no longer refer to intuitively identifiable objects; their legitimacy can be established only in discourse. What is anticipated in these positings, both doxic and otherwise, is not the possibility of the intuitive fulfillment of an intention, but justifiability: that is, the possibility of a consensus, obtained without force, about the legitimacy of the claim in question.

This consideration leads me back once more to Husserl's idea of a life of absolute self-responsibility. If every positing is associated with an interest in redeeming the posited claim to validity, then the fact that the lifeworld rests on a broad foundation of claims that are hardly redeemed, but merely acknowledged, in fact calls for explanation. Until now, our story has treated the ubiquity of naively accepted, unproblematic, and yet unproven assumptions of validity as a basic characteristic of social lifeworlds. Husserl obviously cannot specify an interest that would be powerful enough to effect a persistent and sweeping clarification and enlightenment of all claims. That is why his attempt to unite the task of phenomenology with the need for a philosophical life of absolute self-responsibility retains the character of a powerless postulate.

A communicative theory of society, too, will proceed from the fact that a claim to validity implied in a symbolic utterance can subsist as long as people are convinced of the discursive justifiability of its implied validity, and no longer. But then the fact that the lifeworld is based on a mass of mere de facto claims whose legitimacy has never been problematized or demonstrated becomes a phenomenon requiring explanation. What needs to be explained is how the conviction that validity claims are discursively redeemable comes into being and is stabilized without actual corresponding attempts at discursive justification. For, whenever a claim would not hold up to verification, this naive trust would reveal itself to be false consciousness. Thus we need a theory that explains how the genesis and stabilization of false consciousness is possible, and in particular why ideology formation is necessary. Such an explanation would at the same time be able to answer the question of whether there is an interest in the enlightenment of false consciousness. We can already see that if such an interest in enlightenment could be identified and derived from the conditions of reproduction of a symbolically structured reality, it could not be satisfied by phenomenological reflection on the transcendental history of the genesis of the lifeworld. Rather, it would require a thematization of validity claims that had hitherto escaped testing for not merely contingent, but systematic reasons. Such a thematization would have to have practical consequences.

With this anticipation I have gotten ahead of my argument. I criticized the concept of truth as evidence and showed that the difficulties mentioned can be avoided by replacing the approach of the philosophy of consciousness with that of the philosophy of language. But I have not shown just why this approach should be chosen. This I shall do by examining the second problem that confronts every generative theory of society in addition to the immanent truth relation of a meaningfully structured lifeworld. The attempt to provide a phenomenological foundation of intersubjectivity will show that we are forced to abandon the primacy of intentionality in favor of the priority of mutual linguistic understanding.

Husserl takes himself to be confronted with the following problem. How can I, as a transcendental ego constituting the entirety of my experience, constitute another ego and nevertheless experience what is constituted in me as another ego? As Husserl explicitly says, the philosophy of consciousness starts with the constituting activities of the meditating ego qua monad. Given the assumptions of the philosophy of consciousness, this task is thus clearly paradoxical. On the one hand, it is I who constitutes the other as an element of my world; but as an other, he precisely cannot be given to me originarily in his own constitutive activities, which in principle he would have to be if the other were constituted by me. It must be possible to resolve this paradox with the means available to phenomenology, if only to establish the meaning of an objective world. For the objectivity of the world means that the world is present for everyone as the same world that I constitute for myself. As an objective world, the world that I constitute must be the same as that constituted by all others. Only nature is given to me as objective. I constitute it in modes of givenness that are the same for all others. In this objective world, I can encounter the initially constituted others as empirical subjects:

Accordingly the *intrinsically first other* (the first "non-Ego") *is the other Ego.* And the other Ego makes constitutionally possible a new infinite domain of what is "other": an *Objective Nature* and a whole Objective world, to which all other Egos and I myself belong.[18]

Husserl sees that the meaning of the objectivity of my world does not depend only on the constitution of many other subjects, all of whom are given their own world. It further requires the constitution of a community of all possible subjects, including myself, for whom my world and their worlds are posited identically as our world. He continues in the passage just quoted,

This constitution, arising on the basis of the *"pure"* others (the other Egos who as yet have no worldly sense), is essentially such that the others-for-me do not remain isolated; on the contrary, an *Ego-community*, which includes me, becomes constituted . . . as a community of Egos existing with each other and for each other—*ultimately a community of monads*, which, moreover . . . constitutes the *one identical world. In this world* all Egos again present themselves, but in an *Objectivating apperception* with the sense *"men"* or "psychophysical men as worldly Objects."[19]

Husserl makes the important distinction between an objective world and an intersubjective world; this distinction is also important for a communicative theory of society. The objective world is one in which all natural objects (including other people) can be encountered as innerworldly entities, whereas the intersubjective world is one of transcendentally sociated subjects, who encounter one another at the level of the common constitution of a world that is identical for them and hence objective. This is the social lifeworld, in which subjects can reach mutual understanding with one another about innerworldly matters. "In" their lifeworld, sociated subjects are always already operating "at" the transcendental level of intersubjectivity. Hence they must undergo a change of perspective as soon as one subject is to take another no longer as alter ego, but as a component of objective nature, that is, as an observed body.

In the fifth *Cartesian Meditation* Husserl tries to solve the problem of the phenomenological foundation of intersubjectivity. He has to suppose that the constituting ego has an initial state in which nature is given as radically denuded of all other subjects and all intersubjective relations. This nature can not yet be posited as objective nature. If we abstract in this way from *everything* that is foreign to the ego, we are left with a "primordial" world that only contains what is immediately my (that is, the meditating ego's) own and that presents itself to me in an oddly muted transcendence. Of all the bodies of this "nature reduced to the ego's proper sphere," one alone is distinguished as my body. My living body is the extraordinary body in which I can do as I please while constituting my world. I can ascribe fields of sensation and activity and corresponding kinesthetic phenomena to the organs of my body. Taking this state as his reference point, Husserl constructs the transcendental history of intersubjectivity in two steps.

(a) Experiencing my own body in an originary manner, I first encounter the other within my primordial world as a body. In an analogizing apprehension, I can perceive this body as one similar to my own living body. I perceive it in analogizing apperception as another living body, that is, I interpret it as another living body. In so doing, and conscious of the inner life that is always connected with my body in originary experience, I perform an analogizing transfer: I assume that the other living body is also associated in the same way with an inner life, although this life is not accessible to me *originaliter.* Husserl calls such a presentation, in which something not given is made present, *appresentation.* The living body of the other "appresents" a life of conscious acts that is at first inaccessible and foreign to me. This life of the conscious acts of the other, mediated by his living body, is the absolutely first foreign object that comes into being in my primordial world. This constitutes the meaning of another subject whose body is associated with her as a living body just as my own living body is associated with me.

(b) In the second step of his argument, Husserl tries to make the case that the meaning of the appresentation of the other's inner life unproblematically gives rise to the community [*Vergemeinschaftung*] of monads. He bases his argument on the fact that the spatial perspectives of "here" and "there," which are centered in the living body, are mutually interchangeable and, in this way, can be objectified. I can interpret the other's body on analogy with my own, as though my body here were in the place of the other's body there. Having done this, and inferring from the appresented inner life of the other, I can constitute the other's world on analogy with my own. Husserl now wants to show that, with the constitution of the other, a transcendental We is also formed, to which one and the same nature, and thus an objective nature, is given. To demonstrate this, Husserl appeals to the interchangeability of spatial perspectives. Just as I can virtually occupy the place of the other living body and exchange my Here for its There, so I can also adopt the world perspective of the other who is appresented in that body and relativize the egocentric association of its and my world perspectives in favor of one that is common to both of us. The other's living body

appresents first of all the other Ego's governing in this body, the body over there, and mediately his governing in the Nature that appears to him perceptually—identically the Nature to which the body over there belongs, identically the Nature that is my primordial Nature. It is the same Nature, but in the mode of appearance: "as if I were standing over there, where the Other's body is." . . . *In the appresented other ego* the synthetic systems are *the same*, with all their modes of appearance, accordingly with all the possible perceptions and the noematic contents of these: except that the actual perceptions and the modes of givenness actualized therein, and also in part the objects actually perceived, are *not the same;* rather the objects perceived are precisely those perceivable *from there*, and *as* they are perceivable from there.[20]

The interchangeability or reciprocity of perspectives grounds the identity of my system of appearances with that of the bodily appresented other. At the same time, the transcendental We of communalized monads is constituted in this identity through interchangeability.

I have presented Husserl's account to the point where I can now discuss the two most important objections to it. Both of them indicate that Husserl begs the question of intersubjectivity, which he cannot derive on the assumptions of a philosophy of consciousness.

Against (a): Husserl must be able to give grounds for why, in my primordial world, in which only one body is distinguished as my originarily experienced living body, I should be able to separate out of the totality of all other bodies a subclass of the potential living bodies of other subjects. Husserl justifies the possibility of the apperceptive transfer of my own bodily experience to the other's body by appeal to a perceptible similarity between the two objects. But we could perceive a relation of similarity between my living body and another body only after having objectified my own body as an element of an objective nature. The merely subjectively experienced body is so dissimilar to the perceived body, that it provides no basis for an analogizing transfer.[21] In fact, even Husserl does not rely on a relation of similarity. The attempt to interpret another body as a living body must also be verifiable in the harmonious succession of consecutive appresentations:

The experienced living body of another continues to prove itself as actually a living body, solely in its changing but incessantly "harmonious behavior." Such harmonious behavior (as having a physical side that indicates something psychic appresentatively) must present itself fulfillingly in original experience, and do so throughout the continuous change in behavior from phase to phase. The living body becomes experienced as a pseudo-organism, precisely if there is something discordant about its behavior.[22]

What is meant here by "harmonious behavior"? If, as presupposed, only the observable movements of other physical bodies are given to me, then what result are at best regularities in the succession of physical states, which is true of all bodies in my environment. I cannot derive from this a criterion for distinguishing potential living bodies. If, on the other hand, I understand the behavior of the other's living body as symbolic expression, then the coherence of successive gestures is determined according to rules that institute a symbolic system: that is, rules that determine what physical characteristics are to count as signs, what meanings can be assigned to these signs, and in which contexts of use. Although I am to understand the movements of another body as *gestures* by apprehending them in an analogizing manner, I can do so only if intersubjective knowledge of what the signs are and of the lexicon already exists. In neither case can the mere "harmony" of successive appresentations serve as a criterion for demarcation. My impression is that Husserl deluded himself about the viability of his first argument because, in the concept of appresentation, he tacitly assumed what he wanted to deduce with its aid. In the *Cartesian Meditations* this concept is admitted only in the sense of the diadic association of a perceptible with an imperceptible object. But Husserl implicitly relies on a further meaning suggested in his earlier works, namely *Ideas* and *Logical Investigations.* Appresentation is tacitly conceived as the representation of a meaning by a symbolic expression: in this case, by a corporeal one. However, this representative function, which is specific to language, ought not to be presupposed in attempting to give an account of the origins of an intersubjective relation between me and another subject. For it is this relation that is to make mutual understanding by means of symbols possible in the first place.

Against (b): In the second step of his argument, too, if I am not mistaken, Husserl is guilty of begging the question. He is right in his basic assumption that an intersubjective world of communalized subjects comes into being through the mutual intertwining of perspectives. In this reciprocity, all participants apprehend themselves, others, and nature simultaneously from their own standpoint and from the standpoint of every possible other subject. In this way, the subjects constitute an objective world in common. Note, however, that Husserl develops this construction only to the point where I, the meditating phenomenologist, put myself in the place of the appresented inner life of the other and identify its world with mine. For a common world is constituted only through a symmetrical relationship that allows the other equally to put itself in my place, that is, in place of the inner life that is appresented to it, and identify my world with its. Husserl cannot adequately account for this complete reciprocity since the phenomenological approach begins with the meditating ego, whose subjectivity must always be the ultimate possible horizon of demonstration and verification. This leads inevitably to an asymmetry between myself and any other. During self-observation, the phenomenologist's ego always retains the function of an a priori originary ego [*Ur-Ich*].

The dimensions of "Here" and "There" are used with an ambiguity that is of great consequence for the strategy of Husserl's deduction.

At first "Here" and "There" denote spatial perspectives centered in the living body. I virtually occupy all possible locations. Therefore, even in my primordial world, that is, before the entrance of another ego, I can sever spatial perspectives from their orientation to my living body and objectify them as spatial coordinates. (This is one of the conditions of my being able to apprehend another body on analogy with my own.) Husserl now assumes that the free variation of spatial perspectives also makes possible the interchange of world perspectives, which we must undertake in order to constitute an intersubjective world. He does not realize that he is talking about two different things. The spatial coordinates within which I relativize the bodily spatial perspectives of "Here" and "There" provide a framework only for the monological perception of moving bodies. But as interchangeable world perspectives from which I encounter others and others encounter me within the framework of an intersubjective world, "Here" and "There" take on a different meaning. Only in a metaphorical sense can these be called spatial perspectives. Unlike spatial perspectives, they can be interchanged and objectified as perspectives of a common world only on the assumption of the complete reciprocity of all participating subjects. *Physical* space is replaced by *social* space. Alfred Schütz discerned this weakness:

Even if one accepts Husserl's theory of the constitution of the Other, according to which, by virtue of appresentative transfer, your [living] body, appearing in my primordial sphere, leads to the constitution of your full psychic life and further to the constitution of your transcendental ego for me; even if, unlike Husserl, one admits the assumption that my body appearing in your primordial sphere leads in an analogous manner to the constitution of my full psychic life and my transcendental ego for you; if one assumes all this, still no transcendental community, no transcendental We, is ever established. On the contrary, each transcendental ego has now constituted for himself, as to its being and sense, his world, and in it all other subjects, including myself; but he has constituted them just for himself and not for all other transcendental egos as well.[23]

Even on Husserl's presuppositions, a transcendental community can be established only in an absurd sense: that there are communities for me and communities for others, which do not necessarily coincide. The generation of intersubjectively communalized experience, which is identical for me and all others, cannot be made plausible in this way.

In *The Crisis of the European Sciences* Husserl speaks unequivocally of the "unique sort of philosophical solitude" in which the phenomenologist immerses himself when he performs the *epoché* and abandons the natural attitude:

I am the one who performs the epoché, and, even if there are others, and even if they practice the epoché in direct community with me, [they and] all other human beings with their entire act-life are included, for me, within my epoché, in the world-phenomenon, in my epoché, which is exclusively mine.[24]

This is a fundamental methodological postulate of a philosophy of consciousness whose starting point is solitary reflection on the activities of the individual's own subjectivity. It excludes in principle the possibility that the others constituted by and for me could have exactly the same relation to me that I have to them as my intentional objects. Rather, in the phenomenological attitude, I am methodologically forced to assert myself as the primary and foundational original ego against all other egos that guarantee the intersubjectivity of my world.[25]

Experience that is intersubjectively communalized in the strict sense cannot be conceived without the concept of meaning that is communicated and shared by different subjects. Identical meanings are not formed in the intentional structure of a solitary subject that confronts its world in isolation. For meanings to be identical in any intelligible sense, they must have the same validity for different subjects. To account for the identity of semantic conventions, Wittgenstein proposed the model of a rule that at least two subjects must be able to follow. Mead recommends the model of a role that establishes reciprocally interchangeable expectations about behavior for at least two subjects. Concepts such as "rule" or "role" must be defined from the outset in terms of a relation between subjects. They circumvent the notion of anything like a private consciousness that only subsequently enters into contact with another conscious being. Moreover, the primitive terms are conceived such that the intersubjective relation and the use of symbolic expressions on the part of subjects capable of speech and action originate simultaneously.

Communicative theories enjoy the advantage of being able to take as their starting point the intersubjective relation that constitutive theories attempt in vain to derive from the activity of monadic consciousness. Their task, then, is to give a communication-theoretic account of the subjective experiences, to which each ego has privileged access. The constitution of the objects of possible experience *about* which we communicate with one another must also be accounted for in terms of a theory of ordinary language communication. I should like to discuss this set of problems in terms of Wittgenstein's theory of language games.

III

From a Constitutive Theory to a Communicative Theory of Society (Sellars and Wittgenstein): Communicative and Cognitive Uses of Language

I should like to begin by developing the categorial framework for a communicative theory of society. Here Wittgenstein's concept of a language game will serve as a guide. By contrast, Wilfrid Sellars's quasi-transcendental account of the genesis of intentionality clearly illustrates the limitations that face the theory of consciousness after the linguistic turn. His original views occupy a peculiar intermediary position between a constitutive theory and a communicative theory.

Sellars distinguishes between acts of consciousness that have a sensory or conceptual content (perceptions and judgments), these contents themselves (the objects or states of affairs intended in perceptions and judgments), and existing objects (or things-in-themselves): or, as he calls them, "representings," "contents of representing," and "that which exists simpliciter as so existing." These distinctions are introduced from the perspective of epistemological realism; thus they do not coincide with the concepts of either Kant's or Husserl's transcendental logic. Nevertheless, what Sellars calls "content" and "representings" correspond fairly accurately to Husserl's intentional object and intentional acts, respectively. Sellars wants to explain how it is possible that many individual representings can have one and the same content. For only sameness of meaning [*Bedeutung*] can account for the intersubjectivity of a thought that remains the same thought even if it is thought by different people or by the same person at different times.[1] "What, after all, does it mean to say that content exists 'in' representing?"[2] To answer this question,

Sellars does not simply switch from the level of the philosophy of consciousness to that of philosophy of language. Rather, he proposes to elucidate the relation of acts of consciousness to their conceptual content in terms of the *linguistic model* of the relation of linguistic expressions to their semantic content. This means that Husserl's question of how an object is given in the stream of intentional experiences can be replaced by the question of how a meaning is expressed symbolically by a linguistic sign.[3] The sense in which we talk of "contents of representings" or of "contents existing *in* representings," or of "mental episodes *representing* intensions" is to be elucidated with reference to the sense in which we talk of "meanings *of* expressions," or of "meaning existing *in* expressions," or of "linguistic episodes *standing for or expressing* intensions." Representings and their contents are to interpreted on the model of linguistic expressions and their meanings [*Bedeutungen*]. Intentional acts are to be treated as though there are no intentions [*Intentionen*] whose meaning or intension [*Sinn*], as I posited in the first lecture, cannot always find symbolic expression.

Starting with sentences that can be either true or false, Sellars examines several types of meaning [Sinn]: the meaning of states of affairs that can be represented in declarative sentences and that do or do not obtain; the meaning of universal attributes that appear in the form of predicate expressions and may or may not be exemplified in existing objects; and the meaning of objects that are represented in individual constants or denotations and that may or may not exist.[4] The relation between a linguistic expression and the meaning it symbolizes is called a *semantic relation*. Sellars proposes an elegant way to grasp this semantic relation more precisely. Every expression, whether for states of affairs, general attributes or individuals, can be put in quotation marks in order to indicate that what is meant is not the concrete expression in a given language but rather that *this* expression stands for all conceivable expressions that play a role in comparable languages precisely analogous to the role played by the given expression in "our" language. [Sellars introduces the convention of dot quotes for this purpose. Trans.] In chess we speak of ·the king· in the sense that ·kings· may make certain moves and not others, regardless of the actual physical form the ·kings· may take as pieces or signs. Thus in the sentence, "the wine is red," I can put the predicated adjective ·red· in dot quotes to indicate that "red" in English has the same function as "rot" in German, "rouge" in French, "rosso" in Italian, and so on. The semantic relation holds not between the English word "red" and the class of all red objects, but between it and the abstract meaning (sense) ·redness,· which comes only from the way in which I use the word "red" in English and the uses of expressions analogous to "red" in all other (comparable) languages. Thus here the quotation marks are a metalinguistic device for highlighting how an expression is normally used within a linguistic system. They direct our attention to the uniformly identical meaning for which there are expressions with an analogous role in every comparable language system. ·Socrates is wise· *is* a state of affairs that is rendered in English by the sentence "Socrates is wise" and in L_x by the expression S_x (the same holds for predicates and individual constants). Terms such as ·wise· and ·Socrates· refer to the function that these words have in English and that expression with an analogous role have in comparable languages.

In undertaking this abstraction, Sellars must tacitly rely on the basic hermeneutic experience that every sentence of a natural language must in principle be translatable into every other language. Curiously, however, he uses the concept of the role or function an expression has in a language system without analyzing it further (or even using it in the explicit sense given to these key concepts by Wittgenstein in his analyses of language games). Sellars treats the abstraction of expressions with the same meaning as a logical operation and not as an exercise of hermeneutic skill requiring explanation in the philosophy of language. As I shall show shortly, this has repercussions for his attempt to carry through his own program, for the sake of which he proposes to compare the contents of mental episodes to the meanings of speech episodes.

Sellars gives Husserl's attempt to provide a phenomenological foundation of intersubjectivity a linguistic turn. He wants to show how an intentional idiom, in which we communicate about our desires, thoughts, hopes, and feelings, could have arisen from a language devoid of intentional expressions: in other words, from an empiricist language. His construction is governed by the basic idea that intentional expressions were originally hypothetically introduced as primitive terms of a theory according to which the observable behavioral responses of thinking, feeling, or willing organisms are to be conceived as the final states of specific processes that begin with internal episodes or acts of consciousness (representings). This theory is based on the assumption that observable episodes at the level of linguistic articulation have the same relation to underlying internal episodes (i.e., intentions) that linguistic expressions have to their meanings. Once the theory was discovered, it was so widely corroborated that today it is part of the repertoire of processes of early childhood socialization. The intentional experience of the other's ego, once a theoretical construct, has since become a self-evident, mutually presupposed reality.

I am not interested in examining whether Sellars's construction is consistent in its details. In the present context, what is of interest is only the fictitious state of nature in which, as in Husserl's primordial world, subjects are equipped with a full-fledged conscious life while being deprived of all intersubjective relationships. They have command of a language that can be used descriptively, and that, except for logical constants, allows only terms for observable (spatiotemporally localizable) events. This empiricist language can be used for cognitive ends, such as forming hypotheses about natural events, but not for communicative ends. Sellars has to take this reductionist approach if the initial state is to both exclude interpersonal relations and still allow for the existence of language. This latter condition is necessary because the theory of other minds he postulates is to be constructed on the model of language, which means that it also requires knowledge of semantic relations. I will argue that there is no consistent conception of a language of this sort, severed from its communicative use and thus completely monological.

Sellars's solitary language users must have mastery of the same meanings for words and sentences without having performed a single speech act in relation to another speaker. To separate out such a "non-performatory stratum of linguistic behavior,"[5] that is, the "epistemic function of language as contrasted with its performatory role in interpersonal relationships," Sellars distinguishes between "actions" that can be repeated at any time willingly and consciously, that is, intentionally, and mere "acts" [*Reaktionen*] that occur nonintentionally. Sellars's monological language users may produce only acts, or linguistic events. Since we are attempting to explain the genesis of intentional language, we do not want falsely to presuppose its existence in the monological state. That is why these language users may articulate their intentional experiences, thoughts, feelings, and desires only in "locutionary non-actions," that is, in purely reactive linguistic behavior: "these episodes or 'acts' cannot qualify as actions."[6] On the other hand, even such linguistic behavior must allow the expression of identical meanings. Otherwise even a theoretically imaginative Robinson Crusoe would have no suitable model at his disposal according to which he could come to understand the relation between the observable episodes of the other's ego and the latter's (theoretically postulated) inner episodes. To meet this difficulty, Sellars distinguishes between "rules of performance" and "rules of criticism."[7] Rules according to which we orient our actions establish what we ought to do. Rules of criticism, in contrast, provide only criteria for deciding whether something "ought to be," that is, whether it actually accords with a rule or not. Preserving sameness of meaning or semantic uniformity, and thus the very character of language in the case of monological language use, requires only rules of criticism and not rules of performance. The latter would illicitly introduce into our fictitious state of nature precisely what may not yet appear there—intentions:

Because the thinking out loud, and the mental acts modeled on them, with which we have been concerned, are not actions, we have stressed the distinction between rules of performance and rules of criticism. Non-actions, as well as actions, are subject to rules of criticism, and actions, are subject to rules of criticisms, and the linguistic non-actions we have in mind are no exceptions. Linguistic rules of criticism play a key role in developing, maintaining, and improving our linguistic character, thus ensuring the existence of the semantic uniformities, which are the descriptive core of meaningful speech.[8]

The force of the conceptual strategy that compels Sellars to make these distinctions is understandable, but the distinctions themselves are by no means plausible. I take issue with the claim that semantic uniformities [*Identität von Bedeutungen*] can be secured solely on the basis of monological mastery of the criteria of one's own judgment of linguistic behavior. Moreover, I dispute the idea that it is at all possible to judge whether a given behavior meets the criteria of rule-governed behavior if one does not oneself possess the competence to follow these rules. Let us recall Wittgenstein's famous argument, which rules out the possibility that a solitary subject could follow a rule in isolation:

> To *think* one is obeying a rule is not to obey a rule. Hence it is not possible to obey a rule "privately": otherwise thinking one was obeying a rule would be the same thing as obeying it.[9]

Wittgenstein starts from the idea that the use of the word "rule" is intertwined with the use of the word "same." A subject *A*, if it follows a rule, can do so only in such a way that it follows the same rule regardless of changing contingent circumstances. It is implicit in the meaning of the rule that what *A* takes as the basis of its orientation remains the same. In that case, however, at least one additional subject B must be able to check whether *A* actually is following the presumed rule in the given case. *A* must be in a position to deviate from the rule and make systematic errors. At the same time, *B* must be able to recognize deviations as systematic errors and criticize them. Only if these two conditions are satisfied is the meaning expressed in the rule the same for both subjects—and, of course, not only for these two particular subjects, but for all subjects capable of speech and action who could take on the roles of *A* and *B*.[10]

The point of these reflections is that I myself cannot be sure of whether I am following a rule unless there is a context in which I can *subject my behavior to another's criticism* and we can come to a *consensus*. The other's capacity to criticize presupposes in turn that she has mastery of the same rule-competence that I have. For wherein does the intersubjectivity of the validity of rules consist? *B* can perform the required check of *A*'s rule-governed behavior only if *B* can demonstrate to *A* that, in a given case, *A* has made a mistake: that is, only if *B* can, if necessary, bring about a mutual agreement about the correct application of the rule. For example, *B* can take on *A*'s role and show what *A* has done wrong. In this case, *A* takes on the role of the critic who can now justify her original behavior in turn if she can demonstrate to B that B has misapplied the rule. Without this possibility of *reciprocal critique* and instruction leading to agreement, without the possibility of reaching mutual understanding about the rule according to which both subjects orient their behavior by following it, we could not even speak of "the same" rule at all. Indeed, without the possibility of intersubjective rule-following, a solitary subject could not even have the concept of a rule.

Wittgenstein uses the analysis of the concept of "obeying a rule" to show that understanding sameness of meaning conceptually presupposes the ability to engage in a public practice with at least one other subject, where all participants must have the competence both to behave in rule-governed fashion and critically to evaluate such behavior. An isolated subject who possesses only one of these competencies cannot master semantic conventions.[11]

The monological language users who populate Sellars's state of nature are supposed to know what it means to say that a word or a sentence has a meaning. They are supposed to be in a position to find out by comparison the analogous roles played in different languages by expressions with the same meaning and thus to identify abstract meanings "by comparing the jobs they do with the jobs done by expressions in the base language."[12] Wittgenstein speaks in the same sense of the role taken on by words in language.[13] But Wittgenstein analyzes the language systems within which words (or sentences) can assume comparable functions and shows that these language systems are public in character and always require the interaction of at least two subjects. If Sellars's monological language users actually could identify meanings, they would already be functioning at the level of intersubjective communication. That is to say, they would already be using the very intentional idiom that was to have been derived from the fictitious state of nature. It is true that Sellars avoids Husserl's error of a nonlinguistic intentionalist theory of meaning. But he accepts Wittgenstein's insight that "it is in language [and only in language—J. H.] that an expectation and its fulfillment make contact"[14] only in order to separate language itself from its inherent form: the intersubjectivity of possible mutual understanding. Sellars fails at this paradoxical task of grounding intersubjectivity in monological language just as Husserl did in his analogous attempt—and for similar reasons. As the word "monological" implies, the monological use of language is conceivable only as a limiting case of communicative language use, and not as its possible foundation.

In contrast, Wittgenstein makes the transition from the philosophy of consciousness to the philosophy of language without hesitation. First, he treats intentional contents independently from intentional experiences; they at first have nothing to do with acts of consciousness or inner episodes. It is in language itself that intentions make contact with their fulfillment. As an example Wittgenstein uses a mathematical problem and the operation that solves it: "From expectation to fulfillment is a step in a calculation."[15] The case of sentences is analogous. From an imperative sentence we derive the action that can be regarded as fulfilling the imperative, and from a declarative sentence we can derive the fact that makes it true. Intention and fulfillment belong to the grammar of the sentence:

Insofar as the meaning of words becomes clear in the fulfillment of an expectation, in the satisfaction of a wish, in the carrying out of an order, etc., it already shows itself when we put the expectation into language. It is therefore completely determined in the grammar.[16]

The meaning of the sentence is not pneumatic; it is not explained by relating it to intentions or meaning-giving acts. To the contrary, the meaning of intentions can only be specified with reference to the meaning of sentences: "The meaning of the sentence is not a soul."[17] Something is a sentence only in a language. Thus to understand an intention is to understand the role of a sentence in a linguistic system. But in what sense can we speak here of a system of language?

As we know, Wittgenstein makes use of a model: a language is like a game.[18] He introduces the concept of a game through examples. The first group of examples consists in simple calculations that can be performed with the aid of signs and usage rules for combining signs. The paradigm on which he draws again and again is the series of natural numbers. A further group of examples consist in children's games, which have the advantage that they coordinate the activities of several participants. The third group of examples consists in party games, strategic games such as chess, card games, and so forth. Against the diffuse background of everyday speech and action, the comparison of grammatical rules with the rules of games highlights stereotypical, recurring patterns: These are what Wittgenstein calls *language games*. I now want to show both the advantages of this model for analyzing natural languages as well as the limitations it imposes on linguistic analysis.

The game model calls the analyst's attention to habitualized, linguistically mediated interactions. Wittgenstein neglects the truly linguistic dimension of rules that govern how strings of words are generated in favor of the pragmatic dimension of rules that govern how speakers communicate with one another. Consequently the "grammar" of a language game is not to be confused with the grammar of a language. The former encompasses the rules according to which situations of possible mutual understanding are brought about. The structure of a language game determines how I can use sentences in utterances that can be subject to consensus. Had Wittgenstein developed a theory of language games, it would have had to take the form of a universal pragmatics. Wittgenstein, however, did not even consider this theoretical program, which I shall elaborate and endorse as the basis for a communicative theory of society. He never regarded the grammatical investigation of language games as a theoretical investigation. Rather, he viewed it as an ad hoc procedure that uses indirect messages, that is, theoretically inadmissible descriptions, with the therapeutic intent of making speakers aware of how their language games function. If we take a language game to be a system of rules according to which utterances that can yield a consensus can be formed, then, according to Wittgenstein, the grammar of a language game can be *exhibited* but cannot be *expressed* in the form of a theoretical account.[19] Before returning to this renunciation of theory, I should like to note three ways in which Wittgenstein made the game model fruitful for the analysis of natural languages.

(1) Wittgenstein's primary interest in the game model is the status of the rules of the game and the competence of the players who master such rules. The rules of the game determine what signs are

permitted and what operations may be carried out with these signs. We have to fall back on them when we don't know what a piece (such as a chess piece) or a move with a piece is supposed to "mean." The use theory of meaning, which maintains that the meaning of a word or sentence is the role it plays in the system of a language, is derived from this model. The rules of the game, of course, may be described; but a description does not really capture what the rules do. A player who understands the rules, that is, one who can make moves in the game, need not also be able to describe the rules. The specific nature of a rule is expressed in the competence of someone who masters it rather than in a description. To understand a game is to have a certain kind of know-how. Understanding means mastering a technique. This "mastery" expresses the spontaneity with which one can apply an acquired rule independently and thus also the creativity of producing new instances that count as examples of following the rule. This explains Wittgenstein's interest in the fact that a student who has learned a particular numerical series by ostension has understood the underlying rule when he "knows how to go on by himself." The "and so on" with which the teacher ends a series of numbers that is supposed to exemplify a rule stands for the abstract possibility of performing infinitely many further operations and generating infinitely many additional instances that accord with the rule. The competence that I acquire in learning a rule of a game or a grammatical rule is a generative capacity. Wittgenstein never tires of explaining why the cognitive ability of understanding a rule also requires a practical skill, namely, that of acting according to the rule.

The meaning of a rule is something universal that I can exemplify only through a finite number of cases; thus I can explain it to someone else only through ostensive training. To explain something universal by means of examples, however, is not to get someone to generalize inductively from a finite number of cases. Rather, the student has grasped the universal if and only if he has learned to see in the things shown him only examples of something that can be seen in them. Even a single example can suffice for this: "So it is the rules governing an example that make it an example."[20] The objects or actions that serve as examples are never in and of themselves examples of the rule. Only the application of a rule lets us recognize the universal in the particular. Every application contains *in nuce* a creative moment. The student who has learned a rule has become a potential teacher. For owing to her generative ability, she can herself now create examples: not only new examples, but even fictitious ones.

(2) Another feature of the game model that interests Wittgenstein is the consensus that must exist among the players about what the rules are. The connection of language and practice that is supposed to be expressed by the term "language game" is not exhaustively accounted for by referring to operations that generate strings of symbols according to a rule. When Wittgenstein calls a context of language and activities a "language game," he has in mind actions of a different sort, namely, interactions. Orders, for example, are linguistic utterances that can be fulfilled or violated by actions:

Suppose you came as an explorer into an unknown country with a language quite strange to you. In what circumstances would you say that the people there gave orders, understood them, obeyed them, rebelled against them, and so on? The common behavior of mankind is the system of reference by means of which we interpret an unknown language.[21]

The grammar of a language game governs meaning structures that are embodied in complementary fashion in sentences, bodily expressions such as grimaces and gestures, and actions. Insofar as they are elements of a language game, linguistic utterances are incorporated in interactions.[22] As components of communicative action, linguistic utterances also have the character of actions.

In performing speech acts such as commands, questions, descriptions, or warnings, I not only make use of complementary modes of actions but also participate in a "common behavior [*Handlungsweise*] of humankind." In a context of interaction, speaking and acting subjects are a priori linked by something shared, namely, a consensus about habitualized rules. An anthropologist in a country with an unknown language assumes that the interactions she observes are based on some particular rule. She derives this rule based on a pre-understanding of her own traditions. She can test this hypothesis only by stepping out of her role as observer, at least virtually, and participating herself in the communication that she merely observed at first. Successful participation is the only criterion for assessing the

adequacy of her understanding. If her hypothesis was false, the tacit
consensus accompanying action breaks down. The experience that a
language game "does not function the way I had assumed" is the experience of a disrupted consensus: "That is not agreement in opinions but in form of life."[23] Intersubjective validity for or recognition
by a communicating group thus has a binding character. In discussing the rules of games, Wittgenstein makes this clear: "To obey a
rule, to make a report, to give an order, to play a game of chess, are
customs (uses, institutions)."[24]

(3) Finally, the third aspect of the game model that interests
Wittgenstein is the meaning of constituting a new context. The rules
of a game are established arbitrarily. We can modify old rules to the
point where we can be said to have invented a new game. In so doing,
we need not have any particular purpose or end in mind. Rather, it is
inherent in the concept of a game that, though it may be a boring or
exciting game, a game of chance or of skill, or a game for one or
many players, its end can consist only in being a game. Neither grammatical nor game rules are technical rules that can be determined by
appealing to an end that is to be realized with their aid. Wittgenstein
uses the example of cookery to explain this:

Why don't I call cookery rules arbitrary, and why am I tempted to call the
rules of grammar arbitrary? Because I conceive the concept "cookery" as
defined by the end of cookery, but I do not conceive the concept "language"
as defined by the end of language. You cook badly if you are guided in your
cooking by rules other than the right ones; but if you follow other rules than
those of chess you are playing another game. . . . The connection between
the rules of cookery and the grammar of the word "cook" is not the same as
that between the rules of chess and the expression "play chess" or that between the rules of multiplication and the grammar of the word "multiply."[25]

Like the rules of games, grammatical rules are *constitutive*. For they
do not serve to regulate a form of behavior that exists independently
of them. Rather they create a new category of modes of behavior.
The purpose to which such generative rules can be related is constituted by these rules themselves. Thus we cannot regard language as
an institution that serves a particular purpose, such as reaching mutual understanding. For the concept of language is already contained
in this concept of communication.

Nevertheless, it is precisely the conventional character of the game that shows the limits of attempting to understand language on the model of a game. Wittgenstein himself notes at one point the difference between the arbitrariness of a game upon which we have agreed and the recalcitrance of a language passed down by tradition, whose grammar I must obey. A language is just not simply a game; we have to take it seriously.

Is meaning then really only the use of the word? Isn't it the way this use *meshes with our life?* Isn't its use *part of our life?*[26]

In this passage Wittgenstein expressly distances himself from the idea that the use of language is merely a game or a form of propriety. For me to be able to understand it, "it must mesh with *my own* life."[27] What can this mean? We do not choose the rules of a language in the same arbitrary way in which we do the rules of a game. Precisely in this regard a strategic game like chess is not an appropriate model for language. Two constitutive features of language have no analogue in games of strategy.

(a) Games of strategy are external to the playing subjects, whereas a language permeates the personality structures of the speakers themselves. Because games are set up merely by convention, the rules of the game are exempt from discussion for the duration of play. During the game they cannot at the same time be what the game is about. Nor do the playing subjects change in their abilities while playing; they bring to the game their generalized competence to agree upon rules of the game as such and to act in accordance with them. True, their personality structures belong to the ancillary conditions of the game, but not to the variables that change their values during its course. This is not the case for the grammar of language games and the communicative competence of speakers. Both are implicated in a developmental process during linguistic communication. The grammar of language games changes in the course of cultural transmission, while speakers are formed in the course of their socialization; and both processes take place in the medium of language itself. Precisely because, unlike strategic rules, they are not based on convention, grammatical rules can be continuously made the object of metacommunication. Speaking subjects, however, if they want to understand anything, are at the same time under the constraint of having to draw on their pre-understanding of the situation in which they always already find themselves. For their competence as speakers is itself the result of linguistically mediated interactions. The game model can easily make us forget the fact that the thoroughly symbolically structured personality of speakers is part of the structure of linguistic communication. Speakers and language are integrated in a different and more intimate way than are players and their games. Wittgenstein does not take account of this systematically.

(b) He takes no greater notice of another fact: the grammar of language cannot constitute meanings independently of external constraints, as is the case in the conventional introduction of game rules. Of course, the grammar of a language game cannot be refuted by empirical statements. It does not depend on natural laws; rather, we might say, it is prior to experience. But is the grammar of a language prior to experience in the same way as are the rules of a strategic game? The meaning attributed to a move in a game means nothing outside the context of the game. Language, however, refers to objects in the world. We talk about something that is not in language but in the world. In the context of a game there is nothing we can do that is not part of the game. Unlike sentences, games cannot represent anything. That is why grammatical rules are "constitutive" in a different sense than game rules are: They constitute the possibility of experience. Although they are prior to this possible experience, they are nevertheless not independent of restrictions associated both with invariant features of our biological make-up and with constants of our natural environment:

It is only in normal cases that the use of a word is clearly prescribed; we know, are in no doubt, what to say in this or that case. The more abnormal the case, the more doubtful it becomes what we are to say. And if things were quite different from what they actually are—if there were for instance no characteristic expression of pain, of fear, of joy; if rule became exception and exception rule . . . this would make our normal language games lose their point. The procedure of putting a lump of cheese on a balance and fixing the price by the turn of the scale would lose its point if it frequently happened for such lumps to suddenly grow or shrink for no obvious reason.[28]

This problem arises only for rules that, unlike game rules, constitute not merely an self-contained context of meaning but rather the meaning of objects of possible experience. This difference, too, was not systematically accounted for by Wittgenstein after he abandoned the concept of a universal language that represents the facts and has a transcendental status.

I would like to discuss briefly the two dimensions in which to develop philosophy of language beyond the limits of the game model of language.

Regarding (a), the intersubjective relation between speakers: Wittgenstein reduces sameness of meaning to the intersubjective recognition of rules. But he does not examine the reciprocal relation between the two subjects who accept a rule, for whom a rule, such as a semantic convention, is valid. The fact that each partner must be able to anticipate the other's expectation is by no means trivial. G. H. Mead was the first to analyze this foundation of intentional action.[29] The intersubjectivity of a rule's validity and, hence, sameness of meaning have the same basis: the fact that rule-oriented behavior can be mutually criticized. What this demands, in turn, is not reciprocity of behavior but reciprocity of *expectations* about behavior. *A* must be able to anticipate and identify with *B*'s expectation just as *B* can in relation to *A*. This mutual reflexivity of expectations is the condition in virtue of which both partners can join in the same expectation, identify the expectation that is objectively posited with the rule, and "share" its symbolic meaning. We can call these expectations *intentions*.

Intentions are meaningfully structured expectations that are oriented to identical meanings and whose content can be understood. They may not be taken as simple expectations of a subject. Intentions are not expectations that can become reflexive as soon as they have been made the object of further expectations, whether of the same subject or another. At the level of symbolized meaning, there can be no such "simple" expectations: Expectations are always constituted by the reciprocal reflexivity of expectations. This shows that communication through meaning is possible only on condition of simultaneous metacommunication. Communication by means of shared meanings requires reaching understanding about something and simultaneously reaching understanding about the intersubjective validity of what is being communicated. By means of symbolized meaning, something that is now absent is made present inasmuch as at least two subjects capable of speech and action come to share this representation. Yet it does not suffice to reduce identity of meaning to the reciprocal reflexivity of expectations. For this reciprocity presupposes in turn the *subjects' mutual recognition*. By joining in their expectations, subjects constitute meanings that they can share. Here we must suppose that they themselves were formed as subjects capable of speech and action only in connection with acts of mutual recognition. For it is only their communicative competence, that is, their capacity to speak (and to act), that makes them subjects. From this point of view, intersubjectivity reveals itself as a paradoxical relation.

Insofar as they take the role of subjects, subjects who mutually *recognize* each other as such must regard one another as identical: Each must subsume both herself and the other under the same category. At the same time, however, the relation of *reciprocity* in recognition also requires the nonidentity of ego and other. Indeed, each must affirm her absolute difference from the other. For to be a subject includes the claim to individuation. This dialectic of the ego was first developed by Fichte and Hegel. Obviously one is initiated into the paradoxical relation of intersubjectivity through the system of personal pronouns; Humboldt, in particular, called attention to this. As even Husserl realized, reciprocal reflexivity of expectation, in which identical meanings are constituted, requires that each subject can identify and have an expectation simultaneously from her own position and from that of the other. This requires, in turn, the simultaneous perception of dialogue roles that are incompatible to the extent that a speaking and acting ego can identify with her other as with another ego only if the latter is captured as different from herself, as not identical with herself. Whenever two subjects confront one another at the level of intersubjectivity in order to speak or interact with one another, they master this paradoxical relation. To be able to enter into the paradoxical relation of intersubjectivity that underlies all logically consistent communications, a speaker must have the competence to apply personal pronouns in accordance with rules. She must say "I" to herself, and address the other, who equally can say "I" to himself, as "you." At the same time the two delimit themselves as "we" from all outsiders (from "him" and "them"), who are merely potential participants in conversation.

This intersubjective relation is elaborated in the grammatical form of the elementary unit of speech: the speech act. Paradigm examples of speech acts are "I promise you I will come"; "I advise you to stop that"; "I shall describe to you how you should go"; and so on. In every explicit speech act of the form "Mp," M contains a personal pronoun in the first person as the grammatical subject and a personal pronoun in the second person as the object, as well as a performative verb as the predicate. We use sentences of this form in utterances in order to both generate and represent a relation of intersubjectivity based on mutual recognition. Speech acts are based on reciprocal relations. The roles of asking and answering, affirming and denying, or commanding and obeying are in principle interchangeable. This interchangeability, however, holds only on condition of simultaneously recognizing that individuals who assume dialogue roles are in principle irreplaceable and unique. The success of a speech act depends among other things on speakers entering into an intersubjective relation by using personal pronouns, and this relation makes possible reciprocally the simultaneous assertion of the identity and nonidentity of ego and other. This particular form of intersubjectivity could be elucidated further by investigating the logic of the use of personal pronouns.

Regarding (b), the relation of speech to something in the world: In the *Tractatus* Wittgenstein had investigated the form of a universal language that represented facts. All and only those sentences or propositions [*Sätze*] of the language that are syntactically correct are empirically meaningful. It is to these and only these propositions that facts correspond if the former are true. Thus the universal language was to determine the object domain of possible empirical and scientific propositions of the natural sciences and could have claimed a transcendental status. Apart from the logical difficulties that stood in the way of carrying out this program, one motive above all compelled Wittgenstein to abandon his original position: the discovery of the communicative use of language. Wittgenstein became aware of the pragmatic dimension of speech acts, whereby we produce a manifold of contexts for the possibility of reaching understanding:

> There are . . . countless different kinds of use of what we call "symbols," "words," "sentences". . . New types of language, new language games, as we may say, come into existence, and others become obsolete and get forgotten.[30]

Of course, Wittgenstein was led astray by this insight. The discovery that describing and explaining facts is but one type of speech act among others led Wittgenstein not only to break with the false monopoly of the language game of fact-stating discourse or with "logos as the mark of distinction of language" (Apel). It also led him to succumb to the complementary error of ignoring henceforth the privileged role of cognitive language use. In his catalog of language games the description of an object, physical measurement, and the verification of hypotheses are put on the same level as, for example, commands, offerings of advice, or promises. Wittgenstein does not recognize that only the cognitive use of language opens up the dimension to which *all* speech acts must refer. This can be seen once again in the grammatical form of the elementary unit of speech.

Every elementary utterance of the form "Mp" contains a dependent clause p that expresses the propositional content about which mutual understanding and agreement is to be reached. This double structure of the speech act mirrors the structure of speech in general. There is no mutual understanding unless both interlocutors are operating simultaneously at two levels: (a) the level of intersubjectivity, at which the speaker-hearers speak with one another; and (b) the level of objects or states of affairs about which they communicate with one another. In every speech act, speakers communicate with one another about objects in the world, about things and events, or about persons and their utterances. Without the propositional content "that p," which is expressed in cognitive language use in the form of the assertoric proposition p, even communicative use would be impossible, indeed without content. Wittgenstein's analysis of language games focuses only on the meaning-constituting aspect of language, namely, its use. It neglects its knowledge-constituting aspect, that is, its representational function. The holistic analysis of language games fails to recognize the dual structure of all speech acts and hence the linguistic conditions under which reality is made the object of experience. It is true that the generation of contexts of communication cannot be conceived on the model of possible experience; no more so, however, can the latter be grasped adequately in terms of the communicative aspect of language.

From this point of view it is advisable to reintroduce at the level of linguistic analysis Husserl's distinction between intentional objects or "contents" on the one hand and the "positings" connected with our intentions on the other. The meaning of a speech act consists of its propositional content p (expressed in the dependent clause) and the sense of the mode M of mutual understanding that is sought (expressed in the performative clause). This illocutionary element determines the meaning of the validity that we claim for an utterance. The model of these claims to validity implied in the pragmatic meaning of a speech act is truth value (or what Husserl called doxic positing). The meaning of an assertion qua assertion is that the asserted state of affairs is the case. There are, in addition, other classes of claims to validity (nondoxic positings). Thus the meaning of a promise qua promise is that the speaker will in fact keep an obligation to which she has committed herself. Similarly, it is the meaning of a command qua command that the speaker wants to have her demand fulfilled. These validity claims that a speaker raises by performing speech acts ground intersubjective relations, that is, the facticity of social facts.

I want to distinguish four classes of claims to validity:

(1) *Intelligibility.*[31] With every actual utterance the speaker associates the claim that it can be understood in the given situation. This claim is not redeemed or vindicated if speaker and hearer do not know the same language. Then a hermeneutic effort is required in order to yield semantic clarification.

(2) *Truth.* Assertions and explanations imply a claim to truth. It is not justified if the asserted state of affairs does not obtain. I call this use of language *cognitive*. In cognitive language use we initiate

communication with the goal of communicating something about an objectified reality.

(3) *Sincerity* and (4) *Normative rightness.* All utterances that are expressive in the narrower sense (feelings, desires, expressions of will) imply a claim to sincerity. This claim proves to be false if it turns out that the speaker did not in fact have the intentions that she expressed. All normatively oriented utterances (such as commands, advice, promises, etc.) imply a claim to normative rightness. This claim is not justified if the prevailing norms underlying the utterances cannot be legitimated. I call this use of language *communicative.* Here we refer to something in the world in order to produce specific interpersonal relations.

Communicative language use presupposes cognitive use, whereby we acquire propositional contents, just as, inversely, cognitive use presupposes communicative use, since assertions can only be made by means of constative speech acts. Although a communicative theory of society is immediately concerned with the sedimentations and products of communicative language use, it must do justice to the double, cognitive-communicative structure of speech. Therefore in developing the theory of speech acts I shall at least refer to the constitutive problems that arise in connection with cognitive language use.

Wittgenstein had marked reservations regarding attempts to develop a *theory* of language. The systematic reason for his interpretation of linguistic analysis as a merely therapeutic activity lies in his making an absolute of a single use of language, namely, the communicative. Cognitive language use no longer has any claim to independence. Wittgenstein believed that the plurality of language games that he discovered encompassed all conceivable ways of using words and sentences. He did not realize that it covers but one of several categories of language use.

After introducing his language game model, Wittgenstein, if I am not mistaken, did not offer any justification for his abstention from theory. To be sure, he had ample reason to consider the roads to a transcendental or empiricist or constructivist theory of language impassable. Linguistic transcendentalism, which tries to reconstruct a "language in general" that constitutes the objects of possible experience, ignores noncognitive language use. Linguistic empiricism, which seeks to analyze language by reducing it to observable events or episodes, fails to account for the intersubjective structure of language (as Sellars's artful construction demonstrates). And linguistic constructivism à la Carnap abstains from the outset from analyzing natural languages. There remains one alternative, which has been developed since Wittgenstein in the process of dealing with his antitheoretical analysis of natural languages, namely, the project of a generative theory of language. If we take generative grammar as a model for developing a universal pragmatics, why should we not be able to discover and reconstruct the rule systems according to which we generate contexts of interactions, that is, the symbolic reality of society?

IV

Universal Pragmatics: Reflections on a Theory of Communicative Competence

Wittgenstein's investigations are the result of his reflecting on the activity of analyzing language with therapeutic intent. Had he wanted instead to develop a *theory* of language games, it would have had to take the form of universal pragmatics. For Wittgenstein is not concerned with the grammar of sentences that are used in utterances but rather with the grammar of these utterances themselves: that is, with rules for using sentences in contexts. By the same token, it is not merely a pseudo-linguistic flourish on his part to talk of the grammatical structure of language games. Wittgenstein uses this notion to give expression to the fact that his investigations take place at the level of the logical or conceptual analysis of contexts of meaning and not at the level of an empirically oriented pragmatics. The latter conceives the phenomena of language use within a framework that is not specific to language, regarding them, for example, as modes of behavior controlled by signs or as self-regulated information flows. But not even the theory of action can provide an adequate conceptual framework for a theoretical analysis of language games. Of course, one can say that the grammar of language games consists in rules for the contextually appropriate use of symbolic expressions. But the rules in question are constitutive rules, and it is by these very rules that contexts in which it is possible to use symbolic expressions are produced. The communicative form of life itself depends on the grammar of language games. This point is obscured by the particularistic bent of Wittgenstein's later philosophy; but it comes to the fore as soon as we inquire into the problem of a theory of possible language games. For then we are aiming at reconstructing the system of rules by means of which we generate contexts where we can reach a mutual understanding about objects (and states of affairs). The phenomenological attempt to elucidate the universal structures of the lifeworld returns in the form of an attempt in the philosophy of language to discover and reconstruct the universal structures of the communicative form of life in the universal pragmatics of language games.

Whereas the analysis of the lifeworld follows the model of a constitutive theory of knowledge, the investigation of the communicative form of life (as the condition of all possible language games) follows the model of a universalist generative linguistic analysis. The theory of grammar originated by Noam Chomsky provides such a model—but a model only. That is why I should like to characterize the level at which a universal pragmatics has to be developed by comparing it with the Chomskyan program. This will facilitate my subsequent treatment of the two most important theoretical components of a universal pragmatics: one dealing with the cognitive use of language, the other with its communicative use.

The object of the theory of generative grammar is language, not speech processes (*langue* as opposed to *parole*). The linguistic phenomena immediately accessible to the linguist are ordered expressions that can be employed in speech situations. The aim of the theory is an adequate representation of the system of rules by means of which competent speaker-hearers produce (and understand) strings of such linguistic expressions. Linguistic competence is the capacity to master a system of rules of this sort. It accords with the general competence to follow rules analyzed by Wittgenstein in having the following two features. First, the speaker has the capacity to generate spontaneously what is in principle an unlimited sum of expressions that are syntactically, semantically, and phonetically acceptable in a given language. Second, the speaker is capable of judging whether (and to what extent) an expression is well formed along these three dimensions. With a finite number of elements, every competent speaker can generate and understand an unlimited number of strings of symbols, including ones that have never been uttered previously. Moreover, the speaker can distinguish ad hoc between correctly formed and deviant expressions (and order expressions that are syntactically malformed, unclear, or semantically or phonetically distorted according to the degree to which they are grammatically correct).

This type of judgment made by speakers is indicative of an apparently intuitive or tacit knowledge, which the theory of universal grammar sets out to explicate and reconstruct. The linguist explicates the know-how that competent speakers have at their disposal. The task of the theory of universal grammar is the rational reconstruction of a system of rules that is not yet recognized or theoretically specifiable even though it is already practically mastered and to that extent known. Reconstruction should make it possible to derive a structural description for every relevant expression of a language (this applies to syntactic, semantic, and phonetic structures). Since it is impossible to enumerate all relevant expressions of a language, it is further necessary that the rules of the system be recursively applicable formation rules. A theory that meets both these demands can specify explicitly how all the possible expressions of a language can be related to one another.

Two goals of this theoretical program must at least be mentioned in the present context. The development of generative grammar follows a universalistic research strategy: The reconstructions of rule systems for individual languages are to be effected at increasingly higher levels of generalization until the grammatical universals underlying all individual languages are arrived at. In addition, generative grammar has two levels, that is, it is a transformational grammar. Strings of linguistic expressions are considered surface structures formed from underlying deep structures by means of a set of transformational rules. Every deep structure can then be correlated with a class of surface structures that paraphrase it. This construction has been fairly well corroborated empirically. It can also be used to give a syntactic account of semantic ambiguities.

For our purpose of delimiting universal pragmatics from universal grammar, it is important to explain the sense in which Chomsky, in introducing the concept of linguistic competence, is compelled to perform an idealization. He himself talks of the ideal speaker-hearer:

Linguistic theory is concerned primarily with an ideal speaker-listener, in a completely homogeneous speech community, who knows his language perfectly and is unaffected by such grammatically-irrelevant conditions as memory limitations, distractions, shifts of attention and interest, and errors (random or characteristic) in applying his knowledge of the language in actual performance.[1]

It seems to me that the concept of the ideal speaker is entailed by the concept of the normative validity of grammatical rules and the complementary concept of rule-competence. It is true that grammatical rules do not at all contain ideal postulates, as geometrical rules of measurement, for example, do—such as drawing a perfectly straight line. In principle, postulates of perfection can be fulfilled only approximately under empirical boundary conditions. "Ideal" rule-competence can be claimed for such postulates in a nontrivial sense, for the idealizations are performed by the measuring subjects themselves. In the case of language, however, it is not the speaker who idealizes, but the linguist—and in a trivial sense. The concept of a norm already contains latitude for possible deviations from the norm. The meaning of the normative validity of rules implies that the possibility exists in principle of violating the rule. Nonetheless, in the linguistic reconstruction of the rule system of a language we disregard all the empirical conditions under which grammatical rules can be realized either perfectly, inadequately, or not at all. The linguist posits the fictitious case of the complete and constant fulfillment of postulates (that are fulfillable in principle). Every logical or conceptual analysis of rule systems must operate on this supposition.

There is nothing mysterious about this idealization. But we must distinguish it from the empirical assumption with which Chomsky gives it ontological import. I am referring here to the hypothesis that the linguistic rule system (like the cognitive apparatus in Piaget) develops from a genetic basis through the interaction of biologically conditioned maturational processes and stage-specific stimulus inputs. The child does not undergo a learning process to construct the grammar of his mother tongue merely by learning from the available linguistic data. Rather, guided by innate a priori knowledge of the abstract structure of natural languages in general, he can derive that grammar from the rudimentary linguistic data in his environment by verifying his built-in program of hypotheses.[2] Chomsky uses this assumption of an innate linguistic capacity to support the further assumption that all normally socialized members of a speech community, if they have learned to speak at all, have complete mastery of the system of abstract linguistic rules. In other words, linguistic competence cannot be distributed differentially. By means of these assumptions the ideal speaker obtains a curiously empirical status. And it is for this reason alone that Chomsky sees himself motivated to explain observable linguistic performance in terms of an innate, linguistic competence and external restrictive empirical conditions. For the actual performance of speech acts is distributed over a range at both the individual and group levels, giving evidence of a thoroughly nonhomogeneous speech community. And if linguistic competence is uniformly distributed, then the actual differential distribution must be traced to restrictive conditions. These conditions must account for the imperfect manifestation of underlying knowledge that in itself is perfect. Thus, if we think of linguistic competence as represented by what we call passive knowledge of a language (understanding), then we can explain active linguistic knowledge by psychological variables (such as memory, attention, motivational inhibitions, and so on). These variables selectively determine how the *empirical* speaker can use the supposedly invariant linguistic repertoire that the ideal speaker has at her disposal. This relation between linguistic competence and linguistic performance results from the hypothesis that the linguistic apparatus is innate, and not from linguistic idealizations.

It is for this reason that the sociolinguistic objections that have been raised against Chomsky's position are directed not at the concept of the ideal speaker but at the mistaken assumption that active language use can be explained solely on the basis of linguistic competence and empirical parameters. Sociolinguistic findings support the view, rather, that the application of linguistic competence, too, is governed by rule systems. The strategies of selection from the passively available linguistic repertoire are themselves obviously dependent on rules (or codes) that also are linguistic systems of rules—although they are not grammatical but pragmatic systems. These linguistic codes (to which I shall return) determine the contextually appropriate use of sentences (or nonverbal expressions) in utterances. They are by no means invariant, but instead are distributed according to sociocultural characteristics. But the conceptual analysis of linguistic codes depends on an idealization in the same trivial sense as does grammatical analysis. Every individual code has a corresponding rule-competence, although the latter must always be based on linguistic competence (no one can know a dialect or jargon before having learned a natural language).

The differential distribution of pragmatic competences does not warrant abandoning idealizations; it simply requires different empirical assumptions with regard to how these competences are acquired. Like linguistic competence in the narrower sense (which from now on I shall call grammatical competence), pragmatic competences find their expression in implicit knowledge: in speakers' judgments about the acceptability of linguistic expressions. Wunderlich distinguishes between grammaticality and acceptability as follows:

The former is a property of strings of symbols that are produced as sentences by a grammar; the latter is a property of strings of symbols that occur in contexts and, when uttered, can be evaluated differently by different speakers. Both properties can be theoretically explicated: the former in the grammatical and the latter in the pragmatic part of one's account of language.[3]

I have brought up these points in order to define more precisely the project of a universal pragmatics. Universal pragmatics stands between linguistics on one hand and empirical pragmatics on the other. Linguistics limits itself to linguistic expressions and disregards contexts of their possible use. The theory of linguistic codes on the other hand, which is concerned with the differential modes of language use, presupposes that the contexts in which mutual understanding is possible have already been produced. Just what is the status of these contexts, in which sentences (and nonverbal expressions) can be uttered, remains unexplained. Linguistics does not have to consider them, and within the theory of linguistic codes they count as boundary conditions. Yet the components that recur in every possible speech situation under standard conditions are not extralinguistic elements. The general structures of possible speech enter into the very concept of a linguistic code. They underlie the differential determinations of individual codes. *Obviously in performing speech acts we also performatively produce the conditions that make possible the utterance of sentences in the first place.*

Generating contexts of possible speech certainly means something different than generating grammatically ordered strings of symbols. For speech acts, which we may regard as the elementary units of speech, have simultaneously a linguistic and an institutional meaning: linguistic insofar as they are parts of speech, and institutional insofar as they make possible the contextualization of linguistic expressions. By uttering "I promise you I will come tomorrow," I am not only expressing a promise, I am *making* a promise. This utterance *is* the promise that it also represents. By means of such speech acts we generate general conditions for contextualizing sentences. At the same time, however, these structures are also represented in speech itself—and precisely as the linguistic expressions that we call *pragmatic universals*. A theory of communicative competence must explain what speakers or hearers accomplish by means of pragmatic universals when they use sentences (or nonverbal expressions) in utterances.

The key phenomenon that a universal pragmatics must explain is the peculiar reflexivity of natural languages. It is the basis for the capacity of the competent speaker to paraphrase any expressions of a language in that language itself. A natural language has no metalanguage that is not dependent in turn on an interpretations in that (or another) natural language. Schwayder describes this phenomenon in terms of self-explication:

What is at once most essential to and perplexing about language is that it speaks for itself. In seeing me do whatever it is I may be doing, e.g., shooting at the top of the target, you may not know what I am doing. But if you hear me say something you will there and then come to know what it is I mean to say. My choice of words is calculated to tell you what I mean to do with those words. They speak for themselves. . . . In asking a question, I do not also state that I mean to ask a question; nor when I make a statement, I do not also state that I mean to make that statement. . . . My act is not one of saying what I intend to do; but rather my act . . . must show what I mean to do. This, I think, is part of what underlies Wittgenstein's remark that the assertion shows its sense, and says that things are so.[1]

The performative utterances investigated by Austin[5] are paradigmatic for this self-explicating capacity of language. The grammar of
these speech acts reflects a peculiar double structure, which is the
foundation of the reflexivity of natural languages.

I have already pointed out that a speech act[6] is composed of a
performative clause and a dependent clause with propositional content.[7] The main clause is used in an utterance in order to establish an
intersubjective relation between speakers and hearers. The dependent clause is used in an utterance in order to communicate about objects (or states of affairs). The elementary connection of the
performative clause and the clause with propositional content illustrates the double structure of ordinary language communication:
Communication about objects (or states of affairs) takes place only
on condition of simultaneous metacommunication about the meaning of the use of the dependent clause. A situation where it is possible to reach a mutual understanding requires that at least two
speaker-hearers simultaneously establish communication at *both* levels: at the level of intersubjectivity, where the subjects talk with one
another, and at the level of the objects (or states of affairs) *about*
which they communicate. Universal pragmatics aims at the reconstruction of the rule system that a competent speaker must know if
she is to be able to fulfill this postulate of the simultaneity of communication and metacommunication. I should like to reserve the term
communicative competence for this qualification.[8]

To delineate more sharply the concept of communicative competence, I would like to propose a didactically plausible series of steps
of abstraction. The abstractions begin with concrete uterances. I call
an utterance "concrete" if it is made within a completely determining context. The first step is *sociolinguistic abstraction*. It prescinds
from all those boundary conditions of linguistic rule systems that
vary contingenly and are specific only to individual speaker-hearers,
and retains "utterances in generalized social contexts." The second
step is *universal-pragmatic abstraction*. It prescinds from all spatiotemporally and socially circumscribed contexts and retains only "situated utterances in general." In this way we arrive at the elementary
units of speech. The third abstraction is *linguistic abstraction*, which

prescinds from the performance of speech acts and retains only "linguistic expressions" or sentences. In this way we arrive at the elementary units of language. The fourth step is *logical abstraction,* which disregards all performatively relevant linguistic expressions and retains "assertoric propositions." In this way we arrive at the elementary units for rendering states of affairs.

Utterances in generalized social contexts are the object of sociolinguistics: It takes the form of a theory of pragmatic competences. Its task is reconstructing the linguistic codes according to which competent speakers employ utterances in a contextually appropriate manner according to sociocultural standards. Situated utterances in general that are not specific to a given context are the object of universal pragmatics: It takes the form of a theory of communicative competence. Its task is reconstructing the rule system according to which competent speakers transpose linguistic expressions into utterances. Linguistic expressions (or strings of symbols) are the object of linguistics: It takes the form of a theory of syntactic competence. Its task is reconstructing the rule system according to which competent speakers form and transform sentences. Finally, assertoric propositions [*Aussagen*] are the object of logic. Logic has the task of reconstructing the rule system according to which we form propositions and transform them while preserving their truth-value. Logic prescinds from the embeddedness of assertoric sentences in speech acts. To this extent it deals with both less and more than linguistics. These distinctions give rise to the following correlations:

Object domain	Competence	Theory
utterances in social contexts	pragmatic	sociolinguistics
non-context-specific utterances	communicative	universal pragmatics
linguistic expressions (sentences)	grammatical	linguistics
propositions	logical	formal logic

This overview is intended only to delimit universal pragmatics.[9] Let us turn once again to the double structure of speech acts. Only in constative speech acts do sentences with propositional content take the form of assertoric sentences or propositions. In other types of speech acts, such as questions, commands, warnings, disclosures, and so on, the dependent clauses do not appear in the form of assertoric sentences. They do not render any propositions, yet they have propositional content nonetheless. Nominalized expressions of the form "that p" can be transformed into propositions at any time. This explains how the propositional content can remain the same even if the mode of communication is changed, as when questions are transformed into orders, orders into confessions, or confessions into statements.[10] In this connection we can take up once again the distinction between cognitive and communicative language use and make it more precise. I call the use of constative speech acts, in which propositions must always figure, cognitive, because the performatively established interpersonal relation between speaker and hearer serves the purpose of reaching an understanding about objects (or states of affairs). By contrast, I call communicative the use of language where reaching an understanding about objects (and state of affairs) occurs for the purpose of establishing an interpersonal relationship. The level of communication that is the end in one case is made into a means in the other. In cognitive language use propositional contents are the topic; they are what the communication is *about*. But communicative use mentions propositional contents only in order to establish performatively an intersubjective relation between speaker-hearers. What gives rise to the reflexivity of natural languages is that each use of language implicitly refers to the other.[11]

We are now ready to introduce the pragmatic universals (a) and then to analyze the constitutive role that they play in both the cognitive (b) and communicative (c) use of language.

(a) First, following Wunderlich, I shall list the classes of words (and their grammatical forms) that refer to general structures of the speech situation.

1. Personal pronouns (owning to their double performative and referential function I shall not simply subsume them under singular terms);

2. Words and phrases that are used for the initiation of speech and for address (grammatical form: vocative, honorative);

3. Deictic expressions (of space and time); demonstratives and articles; numerals, quantifiers (grammatical forms: tense, grammatical modes);

4. Performative verbs (grammatical forms: interrogative, imperative);

5. Nonperformative intentional verbs and modal adverbs.

I call these classes of linguistic expressions *pragmatic universals* because they can be correlated with universal structures of the speech situation. Classes 1 and 2 indicate the speaker-hearers and the potential participants in conversation. Class 3 indicates the spatiotemporal and factual elements of the speech situation. Class 4 indicates the relation of the speaker to her utterance, and the relation between speakers and hearers. Class 5, finally, indicates the intentions and experiences of the speaker.

I do not consider it adequate to regard the pragmatic universals as components of a metalanguage in which we can reach an understanding about the elements of the speech situation. This view creates the misleading impression that the universal structures of the speech situation are given as empirical boundary conditions independent of speech. In fact, however, we can employ sentences in utterances only if we ourselves, by means of pragmatic universals, produce the conditions under which communication is possible, thereby producing the speech situation. Without reference to these universals we cannot even define the recurring components of situations of possible speech, namely, the utterances themselves, the interpersonal relations generated between speaker-hearers along with utterances, and the objects about which speaker-hearers communicate with one another.[12] This does not affect the fact that pragmatic universals, at the same time as we use them to produce the speech situation, *also* serve to *represent* it.

In cognitive language use we employ pragmatic universals in such a way as to constitute describable object domains. This role of constituting experience is to be explained by a theory of reference. In communicative language use we employ pragmatic universals in such a way as to establish intersubjective relations performatively. This role is to be explained by a theory of speech acts. In both cases we come upon systems of rules that, unlike grammatical rules, do not merely represent intralinguistic relations. Rather, the universal-pragmatic rule system reveals the restrictions that the external reality of nature and society, on the one hand, and the internal reality of the cognitive and motivational make-up of the human organism, on the other, place on language. In the pragmatic universals we see the interface of language and reality. The describable reality of nature and society is formed in the interplay of language, cognition, and action, which is governed by universal-pragmatic rules. At the same time we ourselves produce the communicative context of the intersubjectively experienced lifeworld through speech acts that are governed by universal-pragmatical rules.

(b) I shall confine myself to but a few brief remarks on the *pragmatics of cognitive language use*. We make two suppositions with regard to propositions that we express in constative speech acts. We suppose the existence of the object about which we make a statement; and we presuppose the truth of the proposition itself, that is, of what we assert about the object. Existence and truth represent the conditions that must be fulfilled if the statement is to represent a fact. The first supposition is justified if both speakers and hearers are able to identify unequivocally the object denoted by the subject expression of a proposition. The second is justified if both speakers and hearers can verify whether what is predicated of the object in the proposition asserted is in fact true of it. The referential expression, be it a singular term or a definite description, can be understood as a specification of how an object can be identified. Together with the predicate expression, it constitutes a proposition that is supposed to correspond to an existing state of affairs. Now I would like to maintain that the pragmatic relations between propositions and reality produced in the cognitive use of language depend on an a priori constitution of the object of possible experience. The pragmatics of cognitive language use shows that any given object domain is structured by particular interconnections between language, cognition, and action.

Our experience as transmitted by our sense organs is either sensory or communicative, in which case it builds on sensory experience. Sensory experience leads to the perception of things, events, or states that we ascribe to things (we see that something is in a certain state). The communicative experience based on sensory experience leads via perceptions to the understanding of persons, utterances, or states that we ascribe to persons (we "see," i.e., understand, that someone is in a certain state). Experiences can have informational content only because and to the extent that they are surprising—that is, to the extent that they disappoint and modify stabilized expectations about objects. This background, which acts as a foil and against which experiences stand out, consists in beliefs (or prejudgments) about objects that we have already experienced. In cognitive language use we put our beliefs in the form of propositions. These in turn appear in a descriptive idiom that, according to its grammatical form, is either a thing-event language or an intentional language (which admits expressions for persons and their utterances in addition to expressions for things and events). If we analyze the grammar of these languages, we come upon categories that a priori structure the object domain of possible experience. To form beliefs about objects or states of affairs that can be disappointed by experience, we must first presuppose objects of possible experience in general, namely, universal structures of an object domain. We impute to our sensory experiences an object domain of moving bodies, and to our communicative experiences an object domain of subjects who express themselves through speech and action. The two domains are of course coordinated with one another. Object domains represent systems of primitive terms that enable us simultaneously both to organize experiences and to formulate beliefs.

In the case of organizing experiences of objects we conceive the primitive terms as cognitive schemata; in formulating beliefs about objects of experience we can represent them as logico-semantic categories. Evidently the connection between these two levels (of experience on the one hand and language on the other) is created by action: specifically, by either instrumental or communicative action.

This can be seen if we examine the use of referential expressions. We denote objects by means of names or definite descriptions. To do this, we have to orient ourselves by characteristic features. That is why we can always replace a name with a definite description. If it is to function pragmatically, the definite description must contain an identifying description of the object. It generally depends on the context which feature is sufficiently characteristic for speakers and hearers to be able to pick out from all possible objects precisely that object which is being discussed. The less we can rely on contexts of pre-understanding, however, the more deictic expressions must bear the burden of denotation. Here we make use of specifying expressions (definite articles: the; demonstratives: this, that), quantifying expressions (numerals; indefinite quantifiers such as some, many, all), as well as spatial and temporal adverbs. At the linguistic level these expressions represent cognitive schemata, namely, substance, quantity, space, and time. These expressions, however, form a functioning denotative system only after they have been interpreted within the framework of a descriptive language (a thing-event language or an intentional language). The identifiable object is categorized in the first case as a moving body (or an aggregate of things, states, or events) and in the second as a person (or as a structured web of persons, states, or utterances). These categories, in terms of which we perceive and understand the identified object, refer to alternative patterns of action.

Things and events move in physically measurable time. The form of the objectivity [*Gegenständlichkeit*] of moving bodies comprises, besides Euclidean space, an abstract continuum of temporal points as the dimension of time measurement. The objects of sensory experience must be identifiable as points in space-time. Persons and utterances move within temporal horizons with biographical and historical reference. The form of the objectivity of persons who express themselves comprises, besides social space (the intersubjective relation between subjects communicating in ordinary language), the perspectives of past and future, which are centered in the present and structure action. The "objects" of communicative experience must be identifiable in their identity as a person or group. This double schematization of time is connected with the fact that, on the one hand, we have experiences of objects that we can manipulate within the functional sphere of instrumental action, while on the other hand, we have experiences of ourselves and of one another when we encounter one another at the level of intersubjectivity as interlocutors. In doubtful cases we must combine deictic expressions with particular actions in order to succeed in identifying an object. The same pronouns and adverbs, such as "this" and "that," "here" and "there," "now" and "then," and "one" and "many," require different actions depending on whether they are applied to things or persons. To identify "this thing here" in case of doubt, I must fall back on the measurement of a spatiotemporal location and (at least) one descriptive observation predicate. To identify "this person here" I have to address her and involve her in interactions of some particular kind. An identity is ascribed to things by those who deal with them. Persons form their own identity in contexts of action. They must be able to say who they are (unless, they are "beside themselves," in which case it becomes questionable in what sense they are still persons). That is why in identifying persons we also rely on the dual performative-demonstrative role of the first-person personal pronoun.

A similar connection between language, cognition, and action is manifest in predication. If I want to establish whether a predicate applies to an object or not, I have to verify whether the object in fact exemplifies the universal attribute expressed by the predicate. If the proposition is formulated in an idiom that contains only observation predicates, then I have to rely on observation. If it is formulated in an intentional idiom, I use interrogation as the most appropriate method of verification. In turn, these methods refer to a particular practice: to the "language game" of physical measurement in the first case and the creation of intersubjective relations in the second. One further category comes into play in the application of predicates to objects of (sensory or communicative) experience: causality. Causality is the fundamental concept according to which we subject the objects of experience to the idea of a lawlike connection: It must be possible to comprehend every event, every utterance, and every state of affairs as the effect of a cause. The supposition of a lawlike connection among things and events, as Peirce has shown, only makes sense within the functional sphere of instrumental action. The corresponding supposition of motives for actions and of action orientations makes sense only with reference to pure communicative action. Dispositional predicates (such as "soluble" or "friendly") are paradigm examples of the causal generalizations that are implicated in the descriptive idiom and that emerge when we verify predications.

The correct use of the denotative system seems to depend on integrating language with cognitive schemata on the one hand and types of action on the other.

(c) *The pragmatics of communicative language use.* I should like to elucidate this by providing a classification of speech acts. The logic of the use of personal pronouns, which I cannot go into at this point, and speech act theory are the two parts of universal pragmatics that are immediately relevant to grounding sociology in philosophy of language. Until now, neither linguists nor analytic philosophers have succeeded in setting up a systematic account of speech acts. However, insofar as we may include among pragmatic universals certain aspects of speech acts, the lexical multiplicity of speech acts that are realized idiolectically by individual speakers must be reducible to a universally valid classification. Searle has identified the following aspects of speech acts in general: the preparatory rule, which determines the conditions of application of a speech act; the propositional content rule, which determines what linguistic expressions are acceptable in the speech act's dependent clauses with propositional content; the sincerity rule, which determines the conditions of seriousness for the performance of the speech act; and finally the essential rule, which determines the pragmatic meaning of the speech act.[13] I shall limit myself to this last aspect and distinguish four classes of speech acts.

The first class of speech acts, which I shall call *communicatives*, serves to express the various aspects of the pragmatic meaning of speech as such. It explicates the meaning of utterances qua utterances. For every speech presupposes a factual pre-understanding about what it means to communicate in language, to understand and to misunderstand utterances, to bring about consensus or to work out a dissensus; that is, about how to use language. Examples are: to say, to express oneself, to speak, to talk, to question, to answer, to reply, to retort, to agree, to contradict, to object, to admit, to mention, to render, to quote, and so on.

The second class of speech acts, which I shall call *constatives,* serves to express the meaning of the cognitive use of sentences. It explicates the meaning of propositions qua propositions. "To assert," the prototypical verb of the assertoric mode, combines two elements that appear separately in the two subclasses of those speech acts. On the one hand, "to assert" belongs to the set of examples including: to describe, to report, to inform, to narrate, to illustrate, to note, to show, to explain, to predict, on so on. These examples represent the assertoric use of propositions. On the other hand, "to assert" belongs to the group of examples including: to affirm, to aver, to contend to deny, to contest, to doubt. These examples illustrate the specific pragmatic meaning of the truth claim of propositions.

The third class of speech acts, which I shall call *representatives* (expressives), serves to express the pragmatic meaning of the speaker's self-representation to an audience. It explicates the meaning of the speaker's bringing to expression his intentions, attitudes, and experiences. The dependent clauses with propositional contents are intentional clauses with verbs such as to know, to think, to believe, to hope, to fear, to love, to hate, to like, to wish, to want, to decide, and so on. Some examples are: to reveal, to disclose, to betray, to confess, to express, to hide, to conceal, to pretend, to obscure, to keep secret, to suppress, to deny (these speech acts appear only in negative form as in: "I will not hide from you that . . .").

The fourth class of speech acts, which I shall call *regulatives,* serves to express the normative meaning of the interpersonal relations that are established. It explicates the meaning of the stance that speaker-hearers take in relation to norms of action. Examples are: to order, to demand, to request, to require, to remind, to forbid, to allow, to suggest, to refuse, to oppose, to commit oneself, to promise, to agree upon, to answer for, to confirm, to endorse, to vouch for, to renounce, to apologize, to forgive, to propose, to decline, to recommend, to accept, to advise, to warn, to encourage, and so on.

There is a further class of speech acts, which is crucial for the performance of institutionally regulated actions, but which does not belong to pragmatic universals per se—although it was what prompted Austin to study the nature of speech acts in the first place. Examples are: to greet, to congratulate, to thank, to felicitate, to condole, to bet, to marry, to become engaged, to baptize, to transgress, to curse, to announce, to publicize, to proclaim, to appoint, to condemn, to acquit, to testify, to vote for, and so on.[14] These speech acts already presuppose institutions, whereas the dialogue-constitutive universals themselves produce general structures of speech situations. Also, many institutional speech acts do not require a dependent clause with propositional content ("I thank you "I appoint you," "I curse you").

Speech acts serve to make three fundamental distinctions that we must master if we want to be able to communicate at all. In philosophy these distinctions have a long tradition: reality and appearance [*Sein und Schein*], essence and accident [*Wesen und Erscheinung*], and is and ought [*Sein und Sollen*] The use of constatives makes possible the distinction of a public world of intersubjectively recognized conceptions from a private world of mere beliefs or opinions (reality and appearance). The use of representatives makes possible a second distinction: between the individuated being [*Wesen*], to whose recognition subjects capable of speech and action reciprocally lay claim, and the linguistic utterances, expressions, and actions in which the subject appears (essence and accident). The use of regulatives makes possible the distinction between empirical regularities, which can be observed, and prevailing norms, which can be intentionally obeyed or violated (is and ought). Finally, those three distinctions, taken together, make possible the central distinction between a "true" (real) and "false" (apparent) consensus. This distinction in turn enters into the pragmatic meaning of speech as such, which we express by means of the first class of speech acts, the *communicatives*. For the meaning of speech as such is obviously that at least two speaker-hearers reach an understanding about something. And they suppose that insofar as they reach a mutual understanding, it leads to a valid consensus.

The correlation of classes of speech acts with distinctions so fundamental that they cannot be further analyzed is meant to lay the groundwork for an attempt at demonstrating the systematic basis of our classification.

V

Truth and Society: The Discursive Redemption of Factual Claims to Validity

Having provided a preliminary clarification of the cognitive and communicative uses of language, I should like to examine the claims to validity that are contained in speech acts. The communicative theory of society whose development I am advocating conceives of the life process of society as a generative process mediated by speech acts. The social reality that emerges from this rests on the facticity of the claims to validity implicit in symbolic objects such as sentences, actions, gestures, traditions, institutions, worldviews, and so on. This nimble facticity of meaning that lays claim to validity conceals as much as it expresses the ultimately physical force of strategic influences and the material force of functional constraints; they can gain permanency only through the medium of acknowledged interpretations. In the third lecture I distinguished four classes of claims to validity: intelligibility, truth, normative rightness, and sincerity. These converge in the single claim to rationality. I am introducing these concepts at the level of universal pragmatics and linking them to the strong assertion that the idealizations contained in the possibility of linguistic communication itself by no means express merely a particular historical form of reason. Rather, the idea of reason, which is differentiated in the various claims to validity, is necessarily built into the way in which the species of talking animals reproduces itself. Insofar as we perform any speech acts at all, we are subject to the inherent imperative of "reason," to use an honorific for the power that I should like to derive from the structure of possible speech. This is the sense in which I take it to be meaningful to talk of the social life process as having an immanent relation to truth.

The paradigm of all claims to validity is propositional *truth*. Even the communicative use of language must presuppose cognitive language use with its truth claims, since standard speech acts always contain propositional contents. We call statements [*Aussagen*] "true" or "false" with regard to the existence of the states of affairs that are represented in assertoric sentences. If a statement represents an actual state of affairs or a fact, we call it true. Assertions are justified or unjustified. By asserting something, I am claiming that the proposition [*Aussage*] that I am asserting is true. Truth is not a property of assertions. Rather, I use constative speech acts such as assertions to raise the validity claim "true" or "false" for a proposition. Thus the metalinguistic statement, "The assertion 'that p' is justified," which means the same as 'p' is true," is not related to the simple statement "that p" or "p" as a premise to a conclusion. The metalinguistic statement simply makes explicit an implicitly raised validity claim.[1] It specifies what we tacitly mean when we make assertions or, by so doing, state propositions. The meaning of truth, therefore, can be explained only with reference to the pragmatics of a specific class of speech acts. What we mean by the truth or falsity of propositions can be shown only by examining the performance of constative speech acts.

Thus universal pragmatics is where we can give an account of the meaning of truth. This sheds light on the inadequacy of the *correspondence theory of truth,* both in its semantic form (associated with Tarski and Carnap) and its traditional ontological form originating with Aristotle.

The explicit formulation of the semantic definition of truth is

(1) s is true if and only if "p" is true

where s is an assertoric sentence that means p.[2] This formulation clearly shows that the semantic conception of truth begs the question of the concept of propositional truth.[3] Tarski can replace (1) with

(2) s is true iff p

only because he assumes the equivalence

(3) p = "p" is true.

The equivalence sign, however, hides the very problem that is at issue. For by "p" I mean a true proposition [*Aussage*] only if I embed the assertoric sentence s in a speech act that takes the form of an assertion. We cannot content ourselves with the equivalence in (3) if we want to give an account of the validity implicit in assertions. Rather we must explicate the claim to validity that we raise in constative speech acts.[4]

The classic attempt to circumvent this problem is the ontological interpretation of the correspondence between propositions and facts as representation [*Abbildung*] (the correspondence theory of truth). This interpretation obviously fails to capture the meaning of truth, since images or copies can be more or less like the original they are supposed to represent, whereas a true proposition cannot be more or less like reality: Truth is not a relative property. (This has been pointed out by Austin as well as Sellars.) The real difficulty of ontological theories of truth, however, is that the correspondence between propositions and facts (or reality as the totality of all facts) can in turn be represented only in propositions. As Peirce demonstrated, we can accord the term "reality" no meaning other than what we mean by the truth of propositions.[5] We can introduce the concept of "reality" only with reference to "true propositions": Reality is the totality of all states of affairs about which true statements are possible. Ontological theories of truth try in vain to go beyond the semantic realm. But only in this realm can the validity claim of speech acts be explicated.

The meaning of truth does not consist in the method of ascertaining truth; nevertheless, the meaning of a validity claim also cannot be determined without recourse to the *possibility* of redeeming, limiting, or rejecting it. That is why the *evidential theory of truth*, the Husserlian version of which we have examined more closely, defines truth with reference to the intuitive fulfillment of an intention. The meaning of truth, according to Husserl, refers to the evidence of the intuition of what is immediately given. I shall not rehearse the arguments that have been advanced by philosophers from Peirce to

Popper and Adorno against this sort of *Ursprungsphilosophie.* In Husserl, the impossibility of the evidential theory of truth emerges in the attempt to prove that there is a nonsensory (or categorial) intuition for universal propositions, in which universals are supposed to be self-evident. But even singular propositions (so-called perceptual judgments) contain at least one universal expression (namely, one of the predicates of disposition, measurement, relation, or sensation allowed in observation languages). The semantic content of such a general term cannot be exhausted by a finite number of particular observations. As Wittgenstein showed with the example of introducing semantic conventions, the meanings of words and sentences connote an element of universality that transcends all possible particular exemplifications. That is why the claim to validity implicit in an assertion cannot be redeemed by empirical evidence. Nevertheless, the validity of empirically meaningful assertions obviously rests on experience. In a certain sense, the validity claim is founded in experiences. We can show what this means by considering the dissonant character of "experiences," which both Gadamer and Popper have emphasized.[6]

Especially Peirce and the pragmatists who followed him have placed epistemological weight on the fact that we learn only from having our expectations disappointed. We speak of experiences in an emphatic sense only if they modify our expectations and compel us to reorient ourselves. We do not notice when our expectations are confirmed. Corroborating experiences are the foundation on which the everyday practice of our lifeworld rests; they provide us with certainty. But certainties are always subjective; they can be upset at any time by dissonant experiences. From the perspective of the believing subject, certainty is the correlate of the actual validity of a belief. To that extent experience—that is, continually corroborating experience—grounds the truth claims raised in constative speech acts. "Grounding" means stabilizing claims qua claims: As long as "experience does not teach us otherwise," we have in fact no plausible cause to doubt a truth claim, even though we know that doubts, when they arise, cannot be resolved by experiences, but only by arguments. Of course, experience can be appealed to in the course of an argument. But the methodological appeal to experience, as in experiments, itself depends on interpretations whose validity can be demonstrated only in discourse. Experiences *support* the truth claims of assertions; we maintain this claim as long as there are no dissonant experiences. But these truth claims can be *redeemed* only trough argument. A claim grounded [*fundiert*] in experience enjoys provisional backing; as soon as it becomes problematic, we can see that a claim grounded in experiences is not yet by any means a justified [*begründet*] claim.

The validity claim of constative speech acts, that is, the truth that we claim propositions to have by asserting them, depends on two conditions. First, it must be grounded in experience; that is, the statement may not conflict with dissonant experience. Second, it must be discursively redeemable; that is, the statement must be able to hold up against all counterarguments and command the assent of all potential participants in a discourse. The first condition must be satisfied to make credible that the second condition *could* be satisfied as required. The meaning of truth implicit in the pragmatics of assertions can be explicated if we specify what is meant by the "discursive redemption" of claims to validity. This is the task of the *consensus theory of truth*. According to this theory, I can attribute a predicate to an object if and only if everyone else who could enter into discourse with me would also attribute the same predicate to the same object. To distinguish true propositions from false ones, I take recourse to the judgment of others—that is, of all others with whom I could ever enter into discourse (including counterfactually all discursive partners whom I could encounter if my life history were coextensive with the history of human kind). The truth condition of propositions is the potential assent of *all* others. Everyone else should be able to convince him- or herself that I am justified in predicating the attribute p of object x and should then be able to agree with me. The universal-pragmatic meaning of truth, therefore, is determined in terms of the demand of reaching a rational consensus. The concept of the discursive redemption of validity claims leads to the concept of rational consensus. Before discussing the aporias that arise from this, I would like to examine the types of validity claims other than truth claims that occur in ordinary language games.

A functioning language game, in which speech acts are coordinated and exchanged, is accompanied by a "background consensus."

This consensus rests on the recognition of at least four claims to validity that competent speakers must raise reciprocally for each of their speech acts: the *intelligibility* of the utterance, the *truth* of its propositional component, the *normative rightness* of its performative component, and the *sincerity* of the intention expressed by the speaker. The course of a communication runs smoothly (on the basis of a socially learned [*eingespielt*] consensus) if speaking and acting subjects

(a) render intelligible the pragmatic meaning of the intersubjective relation (which can be expressed in the form of a performative clause) as well as the meaning of the propositional component of their utterances;

(b) recognize the truth of the proposition stated with the speech act (or the existential presuppositions of the propositional content mentioned therein);

(c) acknowledge the normative rightness of the norm that the given speech act may be regarded as fulfilling; and

(d) do not cast doubt on the sincerity of the subjects involved.

Particular validity claims are thematized only if the functioning of a language game is disturbed and the working background consensus is undermined. This then gives rise to typical questions and answers, which are a normal part of communicative practice. If the intelligibility of an utterance becomes problematic, we ask such questions as, "What do you mean by that?" "How am I to understand that?" "What does that mean?" We call the answers to such questions *interpretations*. If the truth of the propositional content of an utterance becomes problematic, we ask such questions as "Are things as you say?" "Why are they that way and not some other way?" We reply to such questions with *assertions* and *explanations*. If the normative rightness of a speech act or its normative context becomes problematic, we ask such questions as, "Why did you do that?" "Why didn't you behave differently?" To these questions we respond with *justifications*. Finally, if in the context of an interaction we call into doubt another's sincerity, we ask questions such as, "Is he deceiving me?" or "Is she deceiving herself about herself?" These questions, however, are addressed not to the untrustworthy person himself, but rather to third parties. A speaker suspected of being insincere can at best be cross-examined in court or may perhaps "brought to his senses" in analysis.

These four claims to validity are fundamental in that they cannot be reduced to a common denominator. The meaning of intelligibility, normative rightness, and sincerity cannot be reduced to the meaning of truth. We understand what truth is when we grasp the meaning of the claims to validity contained in constative speech acts: The pragmatics of assertion is the key to the concept of truth, whereas the appeal of models such as the correspondence theory, which are located in a different sphere, namely, that of iconic representation, is misleading. Truth is not a relation of resemblance. The same holds for the other classes of validity claims. The intelligibility of an utterance is not a truth relation. Intelligibility is a validity claim that signifies that I have mastery of a specific rule-competence, namely, that I know a natural language. An utterance is intelligible if it is grammatically and pragmatically well formed, so that everyone who has mastered the appropriate rule systems is able to generate the same utterance. Thus what we call "analytic truth" could be understood as a special case of intelligibility, namely, the intelligibility of sentences in formal languages. But intelligibility has nothing to do with "truth." Truth is a relation between sentences and the reality about which we make statements. By contrast, intelligibility is an internal relation between symbolic expressions and the relevant system of rules, according to which we can produce these expressions.

Sincerity is no more a truth relation than is intelligibility. Sincerity is a validity claim connected with speech acts belonging to the class of representatives. It signifies that I sincerely mean the intentions that I express exactly as I have expressed them. A speaker is sincere if she deceives neither herself nor others. Just as "truth" refers to the sense in which I can put forth a proposition, "sincerity" refers to the sense in which I disclose or manifest in front of others a subjective experience to which I have privileged access. As soon as we conceive of sincerity as a relation between the expression of an experience and an inner state qua entity, we have already misunderstood it on analogy with truth. In acts of self-representation, I assert nothing about inner episodes—I make no assertions at all; rather I express something subjective. The complementary misunderstanding, which underlies *disclosure theories of truth,* is no less serious. In these theories (of which Heidegger's is a good example) truth is conceived on the model of sincerity as manifestation or unconcealment. This conception does not do justice to the fact that the cognitive use of language refers to reality.[7]

Compared to intelligibility and sincerity, the claim to normative rightness has received greater attention in philosophical discussions—albeit usually under the title of moral truth. Rightness is a validity claim connected with the class of regulatives. It signifies that it is right to recognize a prevailing norm and that this norm "ought" to have validity. This normative validity has nothing to do with the validity of truth. This is indicated by the fact that normative sentences cannot be derived from descriptive sentences. The oft-repeated objections to the naturalistic fallacy in ethics apply to the difference between rightness and truth. As soon as we conceive of rightness as a relation between a commendation or admonition and an inner entity such as a desire or aversion, we have already misunderstood it on analogy with truth. In acts of motivated choice I no more make assertions about inner episodes than I do in acts of self-representation. Rather I do something right or wrong. Nevertheless, to infer from this that there can be no truth in practical matters would equally be to misconstrue the meaning of Normative validity. By expressing that one norm ought to be preferred to another, I want precisely to exclude the element of arbitrariness: Normative rightness coincides with truth in that both claims can be redeemed only discursively through argumentation and the attainment of rational consensus. Consensus, however, does not mean the same thing in the two cases. The criterion of the truth of propositions is the possibility of universal assent [*Zustimmung*] *to* an opinion, whereas the criterion of the rightness of a commendation or admonition is the possibility of universal agreement [*Übereinstimmung*] *in* an opinion.[8]

Not all of the claims to validity that we have elucidated by way of universal pragmatics with reference to the four classes of speech acts imply that they can be redeemed discursively. The consensus theory of truth, which has to rely on the concept of a discursively attained consensus, is relevant only for claims to truth and to rightness. Claims to sincerity can be redeemed only through actions. Neither interrogations nor analytic conversations between doctor and patient may be considered to be discourses. The case of claims to intelligibility is different. If the background consensus is upset to the point that ad hoc interpretations are no longer adequate, it is advisable to resort to hermeneutic discourse in which different interpretations can be tested and the one that is taken to be correct can be justified. Here too the difference is unmistakable. Claims to truth and to normative rightness function in everyday practice *as claims* that are accepted in light of the possibility that they *could* be discursively redeemed if necessary. Intelligibility, by contrast, is a claim that is in fact redeemed as long as the course of communication proceeds undisturbed; it is not merely an accepted premise; communication that is unintelligible breaks down.

The consensus theory of truth, to which I now return having distinguished the different types of validity claims, picks up on the fact that reaching mutual understanding [*Verständigung*] is a normative concept. Wittgenstein remarks that the concept of reaching understanding is contained in the concept of language. Hence the claim that the purpose of linguistic communication is to reach mutual understanding is analytic. Every act of reaching mutual understanding is confirmed by a rational consensus; otherwise it is not a "real" act of reaching understanding, as we say. Competent speakers know that any de facto consensus attained can be illusory; but their basis for the concept of an illusory (or simply forced) consensus is the concept of a rational consensus. They know that an illusory consensus must be replaced with an actual one if communication is to lead to mutual understanding. As soon as we start communicating, we implicitly declare our desire to reach an understanding with one another about something. If consensus—even about a difference of opinion—can no longer be reasonably expected, communication breaks down. Yet, if reaching understanding is not a descriptive concept, what is the criterion for a rational consensus, as opposed to a contingently established consensus that is not "sound"? A rational consensus, as we have said, is attained through discourse. What do we mean by discourse?

Discourses are events with the goal of justifying cognitive utterances. Cognitive elements such as interpretations, assertions, explanations, and justifications are normal components of everyday lived practice. They fill information gaps. However, as soon as their claims to validity are explicitly called into question, the procuring of further information is no longer simply a problem of dissemination but a problem of epistemic gain. In the case of fundamental problematizations, equalizing information deficits is of no help. Rather, we ask for convincing reasons, and in discourse, we try to reach a shared conviction [*Überzeugung*].

Interpretations, assertions, explanations, and justifications, whose claim to validity was initially naively accepted and then problematized, are transformed through discursively attained justifications. Casuistic interpretations are integrated into interpretive contexts, singular assertions are connected with theoretical statements, explanations are justified with reference to natural laws or norms, and singular justifications of actions are derived from the general justifications of the norms underlying the actions. We engage in *hermeneutic discourse* when contesting the validity of how to interpret expressions within a given linguistic system. We engage in *theoretico-emprical discourse* when verifying the validity of empirically meaningful assertions and of explanations. We engage in *practical discourse* when accounting for the validity of commendations (or admonitions), which refer to the acceptance (or rejection) of certain standards. If what is at issue is determining which linguistic system to select in order to be able to describe a preliminarily identified phenomenon adequately, to capture an existing problem exactly and render it manageable, or even to pick out a knowledge-guiding interest, then we have a special case of a practical discourse at the metalevel.

Substantive arguments have the power rationally to motivate the recognition of a validity claim, though they cannot *force* this recognition simply by way of deduction (or by a methodological appeal to experience). That is, they cannot do so analytically (or empirically).[9] The logic of discourse can give an account of what "rational motivation" means only by contrasting it with "logical necessity." This explanation will have to appeal in a circular fashion to the characteristic unforced force of the better argument—better because it is more convincing. But is it then possible to define the meaning of truth—which differs from mere certainty precisely in its claim to be absolute—by reference to the wobbly foundation of the endeavor to reach consensus discursively? How are we to distinguish a rational from a merely contingently established consensus?

Let us return to the question of the *truth of propositions.* Constative speech acts allow us to claim that propositions are true. They enable us to draw the fundamental distinction between reality and appearance. According to the consensus theory of truth, the condition for redeeming the truth of propositions is the potential assent of *all* other persons. Now, as a matter of fact, there are always only a few persons against whose assent I can check my assertion's claim to validity. The actual assent that I can possibly obtain from a few others is more likely to be endorsed by further judges, the less we and others see any reason to doubt their competence to judge. Therefore we shall restrict the truth condition that has been introduced counterfactually as follows: I may assert *p* if every other *competent* judge would agree with me in this assertion. But what can competence in judgment mean in this context?

Kamlah and Lorenzen have proposed that competent judges must be capable of performing appropriate verification procedures. They must have expert knowledge. But how can we determine what sort of verification procedure is to count as appropriate in a given case and who may claim to be an expert? These questions, too, must be subject to discourse the outcome of which in turn depends on a consensus among the participants. Expertise is no doubt a condition that must be satisfied by a competent judge. But we cannot specify any independent criteria for what counts as "expertise"; deciding on the choice of these criteria itself depends on the outcome of a discourse. That is why, if the assent of a judge is to be the test of my own judgment, I should not like to make his competence depend on his expertise, but simply on whether he is "rational." We cannot escape this dilemma even if we assume that verification procedures appropriate for compelling consensus about the validity of empirically meaningful assertions could be derived from the universal-pragmatic features of descriptive language—or even if we could term "rational" all judges who, for example, are capable of methodical observation and inquiry. For how could we ascertain this competence with any certainty? It is by no means sufficient for someone to act as though she is making an observation or engaging in inquiry. We also expect her to be, for lack of a better word, in possession of her senses—that is, to be accountable for her actions. She must live in the public world of a speech community and must not be an "idiot," that is, incapable of distinguishing between reality and appearance. To be sure, we can tell whether someone is indeed rational only if we speak with her and can count on her in contexts of interaction.

In cases of doubt, whether a consensus is true or false must be decided through discourse. But the outcome of discourse depends in turn on the attainment of a sound consensus. The consensus theory of truth makes us aware that it is not possible to decide on the truth of propositions without reference to the competence of possible judges. This in turn cannot be determined without evaluating the sincerity of their utterances and the rightness of their actions. The idea of true consensus requires that the participants in discourse be able to distinguish reliably between reality and appearance, essence and accident, and is and ought; for only then can they be competent to judge the truth of propositions, the veracity of utterances, and the legitimacy of actions. Yet in none of these three dimensions can we specify a criterion that would allow for an independent assessment of the competence of possible judges or participants in deliberation. Rather, it seems as though the competence to judge itself must be judged on the basis of the very same kind of consensus for whose evaluation criteria are to be found.[10] This circle could be broken only by an ontological theory of truth, but none of these copy or correspondence theories has yet held up under scrutiny.

Were this the case, however, it would be hard to understand why we nonetheless assume in every conversation that we can reach a mutual understanding. In fact we are always confident that we know how to tell a rational consensus from an illusory one. Otherwise we could not tacitly presuppose the sense of speech that is always already accepted at the metacommunicative level and without which ordinary language communication would be meaningless—namely, its rational character. This phenomenon requires explanation.

I would argue that what explains it is that the participants in argumentation mutually *presuppose* something like an ideal speech situation. The defining feature of the ideal speech situation is that any consensus attainable under its conditions can count per se as a rational consensus. My thesis is that only the *anticipation* [*Vorgriff*] *of an ideal speech situation* warrants attaching to any consensus that is in fact attained the claim that it is a rational consensus. At the same time, this anticipation is a critical standard that can also be used to call into question any factually attained consensus and to examine whether it is a sufficient indicator of real mutual understanding. The consensus theory of truth is, it seems to me, superior to all other theories of truth. But even it can break out of the circular movement of argument only if we assume that in every discourse we are mutually required to presuppose an ideal speech situation. Obviously this or a similar anticipation is *necessary* in order to avoid making the discursive redemption of a validity claim depend on a contingently attained consensus. The question remains of whether it is possible to design [*entwerfen*] an ideal speech situation. If, first of all, all speech requires that at least two subjects reach an understanding about something or, if necessary, discursively arrive at mutual understanding about disputed validity claims; if, second, mutual understanding means bringing about a rational consensus; and if, third, a true consensus can be distinguished from false one only by reference to an ideal speech situation—that is, through recourse to an agreement that is conceived counterfactually as though it had come about under ideal conditions—then this idealization must involve an anticipation that we *must* make every time we want to engage in argumentation and that we are also able to make by means of the tools that every speaker has at her disposal by virtue of her communicative competence.

How is it possible to design an ideal speech situation by means of the speech acts that every competent speaker knows how to perform? In terms of distinguishing between a true and a false consensus, we call a speech situation ideal if communication is impeded neither by external contingent forces nor, more importantly, by constraints arising from the structure of communication itself. The ideal speech situation excludes systematic distortion of communication.

Only then is the sole prevailing force the characteristic unforced force of the better argument, which allows assertions to be methodically verified in an expert manner and decisions about practical issues to be rationally motivated.

Only if there is a symmetrical distribution of the opportunities for all possible participants to choose and perform speech acts does the structure of communication itself produce no constraints. Not only are dialogue roles then universally interchangeable, but there is in effect also an equality of opportunities to take on these roles, that is, to perform speech acts. From this general assumption of symmetry we can derive special rules for each of the four classes of speech acts that we have introduced. If all participants in dialogue have the same opportunity to employ communicatives, that is, to initiate communication and continue it through speaking and responding or asking questions and giving answers, then equally distributing opportunities for employing constatives (as well as the subset of regulatives relevant for commending and admonishing)—that is, equally distributing the opportunities to put forth interpretations, assertions, explanations, and justifications and to establish or refute their claims to validity—can be a way of creating a basis on which no prejudice or unexamined belief will remain exempt from thematization and critique in the long run. These determinations are what ideally govern the speech acts that we employ in discourses. However, they do not fully specify the conditions of an ideal speech situation that ensures not only unrestricted, but also nonhegemonic discussion solely in virtue of its situational characteristics—that is, its structure. For the previous definitions do not by themselves guarantee that interlocutors not merely imagine themselves to be engaged in a discourse while they are in fact trapped in communication subject to coercion. We must assume in addition that speakers deceive neither themselves nor others about their intentions. Interestingly enough, therefore, the ideal speech situation requires determinations that refer directly to how contexts of interaction are organized, and only indirectly to discourses. The freeing of discourse from coercive structures of action and interaction, which is required for the ideal speech situation, is apparently conceivable only under conditions of pure communicative action. Therefore, the two other special assumptions refer to rules governing speech acts that we use in interactions.

The ideal speech situation admits only speakers who *as actors* have the same opportunities to use representatives. For only a harmonious reciprocity as to the scope of utterances, which are always individual, and the complementary oscillation between proximity and distance ensure that subjects are transparent to themselves and others in what they actually do and believe and, if necessary, can translate their non-verbal expressions into linguistic utterances. To this reciprocity of unimpaired self-representation there corresponds a complementary reciprocity of expectations about behavior, which rules out privileges in the sense of norms of action that are only unilaterally binding. In turn, this symmetry of entitlements and obligations is guaranteed if interlocutors have equal opportunities to employ regulatives, that is, if the opportunities to command and resist, to allow and forbid, to make and extract promises, and to answer for one's actions and demand that others do so, are equally distributed. Together with the equal opportunity to use communicatives, this ensures the possibility of withdrawing at any time from contexts of interaction and entering into discourses that thematize claims to validity.

The counterfactual conditions of the ideal speech situation can also be conceived of as necessary conditions of an emancipated form of life. For to determine the symmetrical distribution of opportunities to choose and perform speech acts in terms of (a) propositions qua propositions, (b) the speaker's relation to his utterances, and (c) compliance with norms is to recast in linguistic terms what we have traditionally sought to capture in the ideas of truth, freedom, and justice. These terms mutually interpret one another. Taken together, they define a form of life that follows the maxim that all publicly relevant issues are to be dealt with by entering into discourse and that in doing so, we must presuppose that if we were to engage in communication with this intention and persist long enough, we would necessarily arrive at a consensus that would count as a rational consensus.[11]

The idealization of the speech situation is interlocked in a characteristic way with an idealization of the action situation. The concept of "pure communicative action," which I have introduced without justifying it, requires explanation.

Up to now we have distinguished between two forms of communication (or "speech"): *communicative action* (interaction) and *discourse.*

In communicative action, the validity of utterances is naively presupposed in order to exchange information (experiences related to action). In discourse, validity claims that have been problematized become explicit topics of discussion, but no information is exchanged. In discourses we attempt to reestablish or replace an agreement that had existed in communicative action and became problematized. This is the sense in which I spoke of reaching a mutual understanding discursively. The goal of argumentation is to work through a situation that arises through the persistent problematization of validity claims that are naively presupposed in communicative action. This reflexive form of communication leads to a discursively produced, justified agreement (which of course can settle once again into a traditionally pregiven, secondarily habitual agreement).[12]

Communicative action takes place in habitualized and normatively maintained language games. They comprise expressions [*Äusserungen*] from all three categories (sentences, expressions [*Expressionen*], actions), which are not only formed according to rules, but are also connected with one another according to complementarity and substitution rules. Discourse, on the other hand, requires *suspending constraints on action*. This is meant to bracket all motives save that of a cooperative search for truth, and to separate questions of the validity of knowledge from questions of its origins. Second, discourse requires *suspending claims to validity*. This is to make us reserve our judgment regarding the existence of the objects of communicative action (that is, things and events, people and their expressions) and to remain skeptical with regard to states of affairs and norms. In discourse, to use Husserlian terms, we bracket the general thesis of the natural attitude. Thus facts turn into *states of affairs* that may or may not obtain, while norms become *suggestions* that may or may not be right.

In conclusion, I want to elucidate the meaning of normative validity, which is a fundamental concept of the communicative theory of society. The naive validity of norms of action contains a very far-reaching claim. This claim is the source of the counterfactual power that allows prevailing norms to sustain without violence their immunity against continual violations. Let me take as my starting point a phenomenon of which every subject capable of action has an intuitive awareness. If we encounter an other as a subject and not as an opponent, let alone as an object that we can manipulate, we (inevitably) take her to be accountable for her actions. We can only interact with her or, as I have put it, encounter her at the level of intersubjectivity, if we presuppose that under appropriate questioning she could account for her actions. Insofar as we *want* to relate to her as to a subject, we *must* proceed on the assumption that the other *could* tell us why in a given situation she behaved as she did and not otherwise. Thus we perform an idealization, and one that affects us as well, since we see the other subject with the eyes with which we look at ourselves. We suppose that the other, were we to ask her, can give us reasons for her actions just as we believe that we can account for our own actions if asked by another subject. This intuitive knowledge, which in the course of action conceals from itself the status of a supposition (or anticipation), can be broken down into two counterfactual expectations: (a) We expect that actors intentionally obey the norms that they follow. Thus we are incapable of imputing unconscious motives to the other in the course of an interaction.[13] As soon as we make such an imputation we leave the level of intersubjectivity and treat the other as an object *about* which we can communicate with third parties but *with* whom communication has broken down. In addition, this *expectation of intentionality* includes the assumption that all nonverbal expressions can if necessary be transformed into linguistic utterances. (b) We expect that acting subjects obey only those norms that they take to be justified. Thus we are incapable in the course of interaction to expect the other to obey a norm that she would not also recognize as legitimate (if she is obeying it intentionally). Even if a subject is obviously only bowing to an empirically imposed constraint, we impute to her general principles according to which she would justify this behavior, too. This *expectation of legitimacy* also includes the assumption that the only norms (or general principles) that are considered justified in the eyes of acting subjects are those that they are convinced would hold up if necessary under unrestricted and uncoercive discussion.

These two counterfactual expectations contained in the idealization of reciprocally imputed accountability, which is inevitable for actors, refer to a mutual understanding that is in principle attainable in practical discourses. The meaning of the claim to validity of norms of action consists therefore in the promise that the norm-governed behavior of subjects, which is in fact habitual, can be understood as the responsible action of accountable subjects. We presuppose that subjects can say what norm they are obeying *and why* they accept this norm as justified. In so doing, we also suppose that subjects to whom we can discursively demonstrate that they do not meet the two above conditions would abandon the norm in question and change their behavior. We know that institutionalized actions as a rule do not correspond to this *model of pure communicative action,* although we cannot help but always act counterfactually as though this model were realized. On this inevitable fiction rests the humanity of social intercourse among people who are still human, that is, who have not yet become completely alienated from themselves in their self-objectifications.

The status of the unavoidable anticipation of an ideal speech situation (in discourse) and of a model of pure communicative action (in interaction), however, remains unclear. I want to conclude by cautioning against two obvious misunderstandings. The conditions under which arguments actually occur are clearly not the same as those of the ideal speech situation—at least not often or usually. Nevertheless, it is part of the structure of possible speech that in performing speech acts (and actions) we act counterfactually as though the ideal speech situation (or the model of pure communicative action) were not merely fictitious but real—precisely this is what we call a presupposition. Thus the normative foundation of linguistic communication is both anticipated and yet, as an anticipated basis, operative. The formal anticipation of idealized conversation (perhaps as a form of life to be realized in the future?) guarantees the "ultimate" underlying counterfactual mutual agreement, which does not first have to be created, but which must connect potential speaker-hearers a priori. Moreover, reaching a mutual understanding regarding this agreement must not be required if communication is to be at all possible. Thus the concept of the ideal speech situation is not merely a regulative principle in the Kantian sense. For with our first act of linguistic communication we must in fact always already be making this presupposition. On the other hand, the concept of the ideal speech situation is not an existing concept [*existierender Begriff*] in the Hegelian sense. For there is no historical society that corresponds to the form of life that we anticipate in the concept of the ideal speech situation. The ideal situation could best be compared with a transcendental illusion [*Schein*] were it not at the same time a constitutive condition of possible speech instead of an impermissible projection (as in the nonempirical employment of the categories of the understanding). For every possible communication, the anticipation of the ideal speech situation has the significance of a constitutive illusion that is at the same time the prefiguration [*Vorschein*] of a form of life.[14] Of course, we cannot know a priori whether that prefiguration is a mere delusion (subreption)—no matter how unavoidable the presuppositions that give rise to it—or whether the empirical conditions of an even approximate realization of this supposed form of life can be brought about in practice. From this point of view the fundamental norms of possible speech that are built into universal pragmatics contain a practical hypothesis. This hypothesis, which must first be developed and justified in a theory of communicative competence, is the point of departure for a critical theory of society.

Intentions, Conventions, and Linguistic Interactions (1976)

1 Semantic Conventions and Social Conventions

The notions of intentional and norm-regulated action extend the concept of rule-governed behavior in two opposite directions. In contrast, the notion of interpretively mediated interaction comprises both concepts of action and sees their development as complementary. In this essay, I shall discuss two conceptual levels that transcend rule-governed behavior as well as two concepts that are differentiated accordingly. In doing so, I will show how to systematically incorporate concrete action, which I have elsewhere delineated from rule-governed behavior.

One might object that the fundamental concepts of intention and convention, let alone the concept of interpretation, are already implicit in the concept of rule-following. After all, Wittgenstein introduced the concept of a rule in order to conceive of the expression of intentions as a way of following conventions. We do not use intentional expressions such as "to mean" and "to understand," "to want" and "to desire," "to hope" and "to fear" in order to report private states or internal events, nor do we use them to express our subjectivity, to manifest our inner life. Rather, in using these expressions, we rely on intersubjective semantic conventions, which give other participants in interaction the opportunity to test whether we are keeping to the rules of an established language game in a given situation or not. Wittgenstein basically wants to reduce intentions to an understanding of rules, to knowing how to use rules. He elucidates this understanding of rules paradigmatically with the help of simple arithmetic constructions or the application of singular predicates. *S* can behave intentionally insofar as she knows formation rules or semantic conventions.

This yields a semantically abridged concept of the intentionality of actions. The very point of the semantic concept of the intentionality of actions derives from the fact that Wittgenstein implicitly equates semantic conventions with social conventions. He explains the meaning of a rule of arithmetic or of predication not with reference to abstract rule systems according to which we perform calculations or linguistic operations, but with respect to typical contexts of use for such operations. He doesn't really distinguish between a language and the grammar of language games. M. Roche develops the thesis that Wittgensteinians can only treat intentions, rules, and conventions as mutually explanatory primitive terms because they treat semantic conventions and social conventions as interchangeable:

Characteristically, the school of conceptual analysis has seen no tension between intention and convention; according to its view, the latter contains the former and vice versa. Hampshire shares this conception when he writes: "Each convention or rule that I accept is an intention that I indicate"; and "Where there is language use, there must be the intention to follow a convention or rule." In contrast, however, there is the possibility that intentional action can, in a certain sense, be the opposite of conventional action. We have dealt with this possibility in connection with the idea that society "causes" actions by enforcing conventions. At issue here is the possibility that, by explaining our own actions or those of others in terms of conventions, we often tend to abdicate responsibility for them and sometimes even condemn them, while we tend to take responsibility and sometimes approve of actions by interpreting them in terms of fulfilled intentions. . . . At minimum this indicates that there is a conflict between the concepts of intention and convention insofar as the one refers to what we want to do and the other to what we do not want to do.[1]

According to Roche, this confusion arises because philosophers of language are too quick to identify language with society. Conceptual analysis

normally rightly assumes that the analysis of concepts requires an analysis of "language games" and of social "forms of life" (Wittgenstein) or that the analysis of speech acts requires an analysis of social acts (Austin). However, it mistakenly infers from this that conventions governing communication are paradigms of the social conventions that surround them and that language use is related to conventions of communication in the same way as a social action is to social conventions.[2]

I refer to this argument here because it shows that the theory of action exceeds the capacity of the concept of rule-following. One can make a convincing argument that Wittgenstein did not have in mind a theory of action, but of meaning. But philosophers of language, especially those who, like Winch and Hampshire, have made the use theory of meaning the basis for a theory of action, fail to see that the concept of a rule, which has been derived from and analyzed in terms of examples of grammatical and mathematical rules, may well apply to operations that are performed *along with* concrete actions, but is too impoverished for conceptualizing the actions themselves. Winch unhesitatingly transposes the concept of rule-following from the construction of a numerical series and predication to the fulfillment of an intention to act and the following of social conventions. He does not distinguish between grammatical or mathematical rules that determine the meaning of an intelligible expression and rules that govern how concrete actions are produced.

Furthermore, not all rules of action are conventions in the sense of valid—that is, intersubjectively recognized—norms. The rules of instrumental action are not conventional in this sense, nor do rules of strategic action per se enjoy validity in the sense of intersubjective recognition of a normative claim to validity. In addition, both of these types of rules require an attitude oriented to success, not to reaching mutual understanding. The monological application of technologies and strategies rather suggests an analysis that proceeds from the perspective of the individual acting subject; that is, it starts with the subject's intentions. Norms, on the other hand, are obeyed with an attitude that conforms to expectations; hence they suggest an analysis that proceeds from rules for action and derives the intentions of actors from the transformation of norms into motives for action. The medium of linguistic communication can be examined from either of these analytical perspectives; it is not as if, as Roche's remarks would suggest, language always represents a medium for the free expression of one's own intentions and society represents a sphere of externally imposed norms. A speech act can both signify that one is obeying a norm and be used in pursuit of a private interest. However, the primitive notions of intentional action and of norm-governed action do lead to different, and one-sided, conceptualizations of linguistically mediated interaction. The advantage of these action-theoretic approaches over a theory that models behavioral rules on semantic conventions is that they introduce concepts of action that render actions not only intelligible but also explicable either by reference to the intentions of the agent or by reference to the validity of a norm. The operational rules that determine the meaning of symbols structure actions, but they cannot become motives for acting. They have the character of semantic conventions, but not of social conventions that give rise to motives in the form of obligations. We follow such rules (more or less) intentionally, but the intentions [*Intentionen*] with which we form grammatical propositions or mathematical expressions cannot have the *motivating* force of beliefs and purposes [*Absichten*], desires and inclinations, feelings and moods.

2 Intentional Action

It is well known that Brentano took up the concept of *intentionality* in connection with discussions of late Scholasticism, in order to distinguish psychic or mental phenomena from observable physical appearances. Thoughts and experiences are intentional in the sense that they are directed in some particular way toward objects and contents. The sense in question is that in which we direct ourselves toward something we see or mean to pick out, not the sense in which we point a stick at a physical object in order to push it out of the way. The intentional relation of thoughts and experiences to their object is characterized by the fact that what they are *about* is in a way contained in them—it inheres in them. Husserl rendered the concept of intention more precise by defining these inherent objects as noematic contents. That is, he defined them as something conceptual that can be expressed in linguistic meanings. This turned out to be significant for the subsequent linguistic turn of the concept of intentionality.

In a narrower, teleological sense, intention [*Intention*] is understood as the intent [*Absicht*] of a subject who wants to pursue a goal or realize an end: *S* is directed toward or *intends* a state of affairs she wants to bring about. Her action then consists in organizing the means appropriate to bringing about the intended state of affairs. In this teleological schema for action, we call intention the actor's intent or will or purpose of realizing an end. Among an agent's intentions in a broader sense are also her hopes, fears, and expectations, her desires and dispositions, even her emotions: love and hate, anger and shame, disgust, longing, and so on. What these intentions have in common is that they refer to objects or states of affairs—although they do so in different ways. That which they are about in each case can be represented as something that is encountered or takes place in the world. Intentions are about something in the world. We may want, intend, strive for, fear, hope, long for, or be disgusted with the same propositional content, say, that *S* manages to arrive on time for the opening of the new building. The intentions embodied in linguistic or nonlinguistic expressions correspond to propositional attitudes. In a certain sense, propositional contents must thus already be available. Before we can want or long for or be disgusted with something, we must have cognitively appropriated this "something" *in some other way*. Expressing intentions whereby we assume a propositional attitude presupposes that we can refer to an objectified world of things and states of affairs. This cognitive relation to something in the world makes available to us the propositional contents that our intentions, desires, and feelings can be about when we express our subjectivity.

Hence there is a family resemblance between the intentions whereby speakers and actors express their subjectivity and cognitive acts of perceiving and thinking. Hampshire finds a similarity between intentions and beliefs: "To express an intention, or to impute an intention to do something is in many ways like expressing or imputing a belief. . . . Any human mind is the locus of unquestioned and silently formed intentions and of unquestioned and silently formed beliefs." Yet this similarity must not lead to mistaking one thing for another. In Husserl's phenomenological investigations, perceptions and judgments are paradigmatic for intentional acts in general. In the linguistic analyses of Carnap, Chisholm, Sellars, Hintikka, and others, expressions of knowledge and belief provide models for understanding intentional expressions. Thus Chisholm's now classic investigation of intentional language use begins with an analysis of belief-sentences.

There is, however, an important difference between a referential relation to an object about which *S* wants to make a statement (intentionality$_1$) and the expressive relation to a propositional content whereby *S* assumes an attitude toward something (intentionality$_2$). Intentionality$_1$ is determined by the fact that *S* places herself in a cognitive relation to the objectified world and in doing so orients herself toward the validity claim to truth. In contrast, what is characteristic of intentionality$_2$ is that S takes a stance toward a propositional content in such a way that she expresses her subjectivity in doing so. She puts herself in a noncognitive relation to a merely presupposed world without orienting herself to any claim to truth. Assuming an attitude toward a propositional content to express oneself does of course presuppose that S could formulate a proposition about this something in the world and that she can refer to the content of this proposition without orienting herself to its truth claim. Examining belief-sentences is admittedly revealing for neutralizing the truth claim of a proposition p and for separating the propositional content "that p" from the assertoric force of a given statement. If sentences such as

(1)   (I hereby assert:) It is going to rain.

(1′)   I know (see, believe) that it is going to rain.

are uttered by the same speaker in the same situation, we can treat them as equivalent. However,

(1′) I know that it is going to rain.

and

(1″) He knows that it is going to rain.

are not equivalent. Insofar as the cognitive act of knowing or perceiving expressed in the first person can be seen as equivalent to a corresponding constative speech act, it reveals the orientation to a claim to truth that the speaker raises regarding a proposition. The intentionality$_1$ of her attitude to something in the world, which is oriented to truth, as such becomes an element of a further proposition as soon as the intentional sentence in the first person is transformed into a corresponding sentence in the third person. In sentence (1″), the content of the proposition expressed in (1′) becomes neutral with respect to any truth claim. In (1″) the speaker only raises a truth claim regarding the proposition that S claims to know that it will rain, but not (as in [1′]) regarding the proposition that it will rain. In (1″) the utterance made in (1) "It is going to rain" is transformed into the nominalized propositional content "that it is going to rain."

We can read off from third-person belief-sentences how S refers to propositional contents, that is, how she fulfills a necessary condition for placing her subjectivity in relation to propositional contents. Only this relation can be termed intentional in a narrower sense. And this intentionality$_2$ can be read off from the attitude with which S expresses herself, that is, her intentions, desires, inclinations, feelings, and so on by referring to propositional contents. In other words, she interprets her subjectivity in assuming a propositional attitude toward contents. Thus, S's immediate orientation is no longer toward claims to truth but rather toward sincerity: "intentions are something that may be concealed or disguised."

After this preliminary account of the concept of intentionality, I would like to address the teleological schema for action. We call goal-directed behavior intentional if an actor wants to bring about a certain state of affairs in the world by means of it. In a broader sense, however, we can include among the intentions of an agent not only goals, but also desires and emotions. In describing behavior as intentional, we refer to the intentional experiences of the agent. An intentional experience is the subjective taking of a stance toward a propositional content "that p," which is expressed in words or actions. By ascribing an intention to an agent, we presuppose that:

(i)   propositional contents are available to the agent, i.e., that he has a determinate cognitive representation of a reality that, for him, is objectively given;

(ii)   the agent takes a stance toward the propositional contents whereby he places his subjectivity in a particular noncognitive relation to reality.

By describing a behavior as an intentional action, we take the perspective of the actor himself; but this agent's point of view signifies a two-tiered intentional relation to something in the world, namely, the relation to the cognitive representation of reality that is valid for the agent and to the subjective attitude that the agent takes toward this representation of reality.

The two-tiered nature of the intentional relation to something in the world is implicit in the language we use to describe a behavior as an intentional action. It has no ontological significance. Brentano wanted to use the concept of intentionality to delimit the ontological domains of the psychological and the physical. Yet the choice of action-theoretic concepts implies the delimitation of object domains at the level of methodology.

The linguistic turn in discussions of intentionality is characterized by the idea that intentional experiences must admit of symbolic expression. This means that S cannot, strictly speaking, act intentionally unless she is able to express her intention in the right circumstances. She must have a mastery of an intentional idiom in which she could describe her situation from her engaged perspective.

This thesis arises from the logic of explanation on which we rely at least implicitly in describing behavior as intentional action. We explain an intentional action by citing the intentional experience of the agent as a motive, as a purpose or intention, a tendency or disposition to react to something in a certain way, a feeling or affective perception of something, a mood, a sensory stimulation, and so on. These intentional experiences (intentions, needs, feelings) cannot be identified independently of their propositional contents. This means that intentional experiences do not correspond to the logical type of events that can be characterized independently of the action they cause. This relation between an intention and the action expressing it is not contingent and is produced through the agent's interpretation of his situation. In understanding the agent's intention as the motive or cause of a corresponding action, we treat his interpretation of his situation as constitutive of the behavior under an intentional description. We thereby presuppose that the agent himself has at his disposal an intentional idiom in which he can describe his situation and formulate his intentions explicitly (given the right circumstances). Insofar as we are following the explanatory logic for intentional action, we presuppose that the agent has a mastery of an intentional idiom. I shall return to this connection between intentionality and language.

First, however, I would like to address the question of whether and in what sense intentions may be seen as causes of actions. Late Wittgensteinians such as Peters, Melden, and Winch have derived a kind of dualism from the fact that actions and the intentions they express are necessarily, that is, internally related. According to this dualism, causal explanation is inadequate to account for intentional actions. Charles Taylor has presented a fundamental critique of this thesis. He starts from a teleological model of action:

End: *S* wants to bring about state of affairs *A;*

Means: *S* knows that *A* will not occur in the given situation unless action *p* is performed;

Choice of Means: Situation *x* is the case; hence *S* undertakes action *p*.

For example, *S* wants to become the next head of government. She knows that a traditional ministerial portfolio is a good position from which to compete against other candidates. Therefore, she seeks to obtain such a portfolio during the next cabinet shuffle. A practical syllogism of this sort can be a reason for *S*'s choice of action *p* as an instrumental means. Of course this *reason* can take on the role of a *cause* only on the assumption that *S* takes it to be a motive for action. *S* must have the goal or intention or willingness to bring about *A*. If *S* has set herself a certain goal, then the intention to attain this goal can causally explain a corresponding action. For the reference to an intention indicates why *S* acts thus and not otherwise. The act of setting a goal plays the same methodological role for intentional action as a physical cause plays for a corresponding event. Thus one might try to make *S* do a certain action by getting her to have a corresponding intention. This can be done by means of argument, persuasion, or by changing the situation. Moreover, knowing an intention can be used to predict future actions just as knowing the physical cause can be used to predict future events.

The teleological model allows ends to be viewed as causes of action if we may presuppose that *S* acts with the goal of bringing about the state of affairs in question. Setting this goal is an intention whereby *S* assumes an attitude toward a propositional content in such a way that the state of affairs expressed by the propositional content is recognized as a possible state of the world that can obtain under specific conditions and that can be brought about by effecting these conditions. Phenomena such as intending, desiring, or willing to do something, however, are themselves in need of explanation. The teleological account in terms of ends that presupposes corresponding intentions is but the first step in an explanation of motivation. Taylor analyzes two further steps: an account in terms of desires and dispositions and an explanation in terms of emotions, that is, of feelings and moods.[3]

An explanation of S's intention to become head of government might be sought in the general disposition to seek recognition, or in the concrete desire finally to outdo a friend who has always been ahead of S, that is, in ambition or envy. One might explain the fact that S made her decision at a time when no one expected her to do so in terms of strong emotional motives: the anger at a humiliation S suffered at the hands of a rival, a peculiar euphoric mood S has been in ever since she successfully underwent surgery, and so on. In any case, we fall back on needs and wants, that is, on motives that lie deeper than intentions or decisions. Needs are Janus-faced: They are differentiated on one hand into dispositions and desires (the volitional perspective) and into feelings and moods on the other (the perceptual perspective). Dispositions and desires are oriented toward situations of want satisfaction; feelings and moods perceive objecs in the light of our wants. Our *Bedürfnisnatur* is the background of a partiality that steers subjects to take a stance toward reality, toward the propositional contents that are cognitively available to them. This partiality guides both how we actively influence and how we affectively perceive situations that are thematized as components of our lifeworld rather than as an objectified Something in the world. Desires and wants dispose one to choose goals of action; feelings and moods evaluate situations and open up perspectives on possible goals of action. Desires and wants presuppose the evaluation of desirable or undesirable states of affairs, whereas emotions and moods have a dispositional element.

The connection between dispositions and emotions becomes clearer if we conceive of both as *interpretations of underlying wants and needs*. Need interpretations involve both feelings and desires. For desires are interpreted indirectly, on the one hand by means of action preferences or *ends,* and on the other hand by means of affectively loaded categories and situations, that is, by means of *values.* Ends and values are mutually interpreting. To specify what expressions such as "beautiful," "terrible," "happy," or "horrible" mean in a given context, we can refer to individual objects or situations that are plausible as possible goals of action. To render plausible the choice of particular ends, we can in turn appeal to accepted values. This mutual interpretation of ends against the background of values and of values by means of ends can be informative because ends tend to characterize particular states of affairs whereas cultural values tend to express something universal. Moreover, the descriptive component is more pronounced in ends, and the evaluative more in values. I shall return below to this dual descriptive-evaluative content of expressions interpreting needs and wants.

But first I want to show how the concept of intentional action characterizes motives as "final" causes. Within this framework it is not possible to treat motives (i.e., feelings and desires) themselves or the needs they interpret as phenomena requiring explanation. The explanation of intentional action may be reducible via ends and intentions to desires and dispositions and, ultimately, to feelings and moods. Yet the chain of explanation ends with motives, however "deeply" rooted they may be. As long as we are describing behavior as intentional action, motives are basic. As soon as we understand the needs of individuals in turn as the result of a process of interpretation, we disrupt the monological model of action of a subject expressing intentional experiences. It is natural to suppose that need interpretations depend on cultural values and on norms that embody such values. However, we cannot reduce an agent's intentions to the social reality of norms and values by way of the process of motive formation without abandoning the concept of intentional action. Thus expressions of monologically minded subjects acting intentionally are replaced with interaction—governed by intersubjectively recognized norms and values—among subjects acting so as to conform to expectations. This presupposes a causal connection between cultural traditions and needs, and between institutionalized values and dispositions. This empirical connection, however, fails to capture the internal connection between reasons and motives, which is the only admissible connection in the context of intentional action more narrowly construed.

3 Fulfilling Norms

The specific concept of norm-governed or value-oriented action developed by Parsons, which has become de rigueur in sociology, counts on a sphere of linguistic intersubjectivity that is independent from the subjectivity of an experiencing subject. Not only matters of theoretical knowledge, but also values and norms are "shared" in this sphere. This sharing or "having in common" is made possible through communication, that is, through mutual understanding that is reached on the basis of validity claims that are recognized by subjects capable of speech and action. The concept of intentional action already presupposes that cognitive acts make reference to truth; and the teleological model of action counts on there being an acting subject that can be motivated by reasons or practical syllogisms. Yet within the framework of the concept of intentionality, truth is not understood as a validity claim that grounds intersubjectivity. The claim to truth can be reinterpreted monologically so as to fit into the conceptual framework of the subjective mind. The concept of value-oriented action, on the other hand, introduces a second validity claim. It presupposes the normative validity of values and rules of action. And this validity claim cannot be interpreted without reference to intersubjective recognition—a monological reinterpretation in this instance is all but impossible.

As I cannot yet at this point undertake the task of a systematic explication of the meaning of validity claims, I shall proceed by way of a critique of the basic principles underlying empiricist ethics. Ethics deals with the same questions from the normative perspective of justifying actions as the theory of action does from the perspective of explaining them. The question, "Why should S in situation x perform action a_1 rather than any of a_2, a_3, . . . or a_n?" calls for giving (at least) one reason. Similarly, it is possible to answer the question "Why did S in situation x perform action a_1 (rather than a_2, a_3, . . . or a_n)?" with an explanation that cites a reason as motive. Ethics deals with a specific class of actions, namely, those whose choice can be evaluated as morally good or correct. The explication of reasons for morally relevant actions must therefore take account of the sense of *ought* implicit in this way of asking the question. Every ethics is faced with the task of reconstructing the nondescriptive content of our notions of values and norms. An empiricist ethics, which is committed to the teleological model of action and hence to a subjectivist representation of intentional action, faces the special difficulty of reducing valuations, which by its own lights are far from merely subjective, to what are ultimately private needs. Empiricism bases the justification of morally relevant actions on the wants and needs of an actor who is herself the final judge of what her wants and needs are:

By an empiricist position I mean the idea that the ultimate grounds of one's factual beliefs about the external world are propositions about what one directly perceives. The parallels between such a position and the accounts of reasons-for-acting are: first, the idea that in any chain of reasons there must always be a point at which one has to stop, i.e., there are always ultimate reasons; second, the idea that these ultimate reasons must all share some common characteristic(s); third, the idea that the characteristics possessed by the ultimate reasons must be such that they cannot be questioned further, and therefore no further reasons are needed, i.e., the ultimate reasons must be such that they can constitute "foundations"; and fourth, the idea that such reasons are provided by first-person psychological statements, since these cannot be questioned further and cannot be doubted.[4]

Richard Norman shows that neither the emotivist recourse to brute attitudes, wants, or feelings nor the decisionist recourse to ultimate decisions suffices for justifying a morally relevant action. Only such reasons are acceptable as make clear why the agent in a given situation has precisely this feeling or that disposition, or why she has the intention to accomplish precisely this goal. The mere assertion that S in a given situation has certain intentional experiences lacks any practical justificatory force so long is it is not plausible that people other than S in such situations also have experiences of this sort that motivate their actions in this way. A want is only an *intelligible* motive if it is interpreted so that it makes sense to others:

To want *simply* a saucer of mud is irrational, because some further reason is needed for wanting it. To want a saucer of mud because one wants to enjoy

its rich river-smell is rational. No further reason is needed for wanting to enjoy the rich river-smell, for to characterize what is wanted as "to enjoy the
rich river-smell" is itself to give an acceptable reason for wanting it, and
therefore this want is rational.[5]

The reference to the "rich river-smell" interprets a somewhat peculiar want. If the desire for a handful of mud does not make sense under this interpretation and continues to seem like something private,
inscrutable, and idiosyncratic, then we will take the actions or fanta-
sies motivated by this desire to be abnormal and may perhaps look
for pathological explanations. Against the background of this example, the specific achievement of evaluative expressions by which we
interpret needs and wants stands out. In characterizing an object or a
situation as rich, pungent, stimulating, terrific, uplifting, successful,
happy, dangerous, forbidding, terrifying, revolting, and so on, we are
trying to make sense of a certain attitude to this object or situation by
appealing to universal standards of evaluation. To the extent that
these standards of evaluation, or values, for short, are recognized by
others, and to the extent that the need interpretations are shared by
others, we can justify the corresponding desires or feelings, and the
actions they motivate, with such need interpretations. Evaluative expressions have justificatory power if and to the extent that they can
characterize a want such that others recognize their own wants under
this interpretation. A want will be acceptable as a reason for an action insofar as the cultural values to which we appeal in interpreting
the want are recognized.

Norman gives the following example:

A proposed road scheme might be very much to a particular individual's
own disadvantage, involving the destruction of the whole of his front garden, thus depriving him of the opportunity to engage in his favorite hobby
of gardening, destroying his beautiful rose beds, ruining the whole appearance of the front of the house, and bringing the noise and the fumes of the
traffic right up to his front doorstep. But if asked for his assessment of the
merits of the scheme, he might nevertheless say that he thought it was the
best possible one in the circumstances, since it would enable people to
travel more easily and in greater comfort, cut down the number of acci-
dents, and cause the least overall inconveniece. . . . This, however, is not
what I have been referring to in emphasizing the necessary publicity of standards. In my sense, the man is employing public standards just as much

when he adopts the former of the two points of view. This can be seen from the kind of vocabulary he might use. Insofar as he refers to the notion of "peace and quiet," disturbance caused by noise, the choking stench of traffic fumes, the enjoyment of a hobby, the beauty of flowers, etc., he is invoking publicly shared concepts and public standards of evaluation. It is because he does so that we can describe as "rational," his potential objections to the road scheme from the point of view of his private wants and interests.[6]

The example is meant to support the thesis that motives for action can take on the role of moral-practical reasons only insofar as they represent *publicly interpreted wants* rather than any private features of the acting subject. What a particular individual wants or desires or feels is logically dependent on the interpretation of the underlying want that prevails in the given linguistic community.

Norman fails to distinguish clearly the intelligibility of an *evaluative* expression and the *normative* binding nature of a corresponding standard of value. By assessing the consequences of the projected destruction of his front lawn by means of evaluative expressions for, for example, the beauty of the rose beds, the pleasure of working in the garden, the grand façade of the house, the unbearable noise and stench of the traffic, the resident provides a persuasive representation of his interests that would be violated by implementing the communal traffic plan. He chooses interpretations under which *others* can recognize their own wants and needs if they put themselves in his situation. His need interpretations make intelligible why someone in this situation would oppose such a plan. But a plausible want or need falls short of justifying an action that is motivated by it, such as a complaint to the city government. The person who is affected may be able to represent his personal interests in an intelligible and plausible fashion, as our example shows, and yet he may place the more general interests of the neighborhood or of all the drivers first. He may refrain from trying to oppose the city plan by legal means, for example. The evaluative expressions that occur in need interpretations render an intention, a desire, or a feeling intelligible because they relate these motives to the cultural values that are shared in a linguistic community. Yet a plausible motive does not yet amount to a justification for an appropriately motivated action. An action can only be justified with reference to norms that lay down that certain values *ought* to receive primary consideration in certain circumstances.

A strictly normative validity that can be binding for motives for action accrues to values only if they are embodied in norms. And the embodiment of values in norms signifies that in situations in which this regulation is valid, *everyone* is justified in orienting herself toward certain values and to base her actions on the wants and needs interpreted in these values. To say that a norm is valid is to say that it claims to express a universalizable interest and to deserve the consent of all those affected. Cultural values per se cannot raise this kind of a claim to validity. However, they are candidates for being embodied in norms, that is, for becoming universally binding in certain circumstances. In the light of cultural values, the wants of one individual are also intelligible to other individuals who stand in the same cultural tradition. But wants and needs that are interpreted as plausible are transformed into legitimate motives for action only by making the corresponding values normatively binding in certain circumstances and for certain groups.

The basic moral-practical predicates such as "correct" or "just" or "good" refer to this sense of ought implicit in an intersubjectively binding norm of action. The "validity" of a norm means the unforced recognition of its validity claim. This claim in turn consists in the claim that all those affected have good reason to consent to the norm because it expresses their common interest. The most general norms that express the common interest of all human beings are called "moral." Thus the idea of the moral-practical justification of an action in the end refers to the idea of a universal agreement that is motivated by reasons and reasons alone:

To engage in the defense of a line of action . . . is to imply that the members of one's audience have certain characteristics which make their opinions worth taking into account. It is, in particular, to assume that they can understand one's presentation, and are able to respond with intelligible criticism. But this in turn means that one concedes a potential (at very least) of practical reasoning on their parts. To see, in the light of this, why "the dice of reason are loaded in favor of the general interest," we can reflect that it would be absurd (i.e., pointless) to raise questions and make defenses of one's acts to other people, if one were not prepared to acknowledge similar weight to similar claims on their parts. . . . There is no point in being prepared to argue if one doesn't envisage any possible terms of settlement; and one cannot hope for settlement if one's "arguments" are going to be arbitrarily loaded in favor of oneself. . . . To argue for morality at all is to claim the assent of all rational beings. But the only principle mutually acceptable to all rational beings is one which regards all of their interests as equally worth satisfying (less, therefore, those which are incompatible with others). Everyone can agree to this because everyone's interests are respected.[7]

These reflections serve as a bridge to the concept of norm-governed action. This can be done by a step-by-step revision. First, the *Bedürfnisnatur,* in which the intentions of a subject who takes a stance are rooted, is divested of its subjective character. Wants always appear under some interpretation that presupposes (a) a linguistic community, (b) a language containing evaluative expressions, and (c) an intersubjectively shared tradition of cultural values. Next, values can be shown to represent something like candidates for embodying norms. Values become normatively binding if a consensus arises among members of a group about certain situation-specific value-orientations. Corresponding to this model of action, there is an explanatory strategy that admits the reasons for an action as an agent's motives only insofar as they are connected with cultural values through the need interpretations and with intersubjectively recognized norms through the cultural values. Instead of private wants and needs, public norms take on the role of the explanans. The values by which the agents orient themselves are institutionalized in these norms. Valid norms have the power to motivate actions because the values they embody—and hence about which consensus can be reached—represent the standards according to which the needs and wants are interpreted and developed into dispositions by means of linguistically mediated learning processes. This is the basic outline of the model that Parsons constructed based on the concept of a norm and of conformity with norms.

Just as we connect theories to a claim to truth, so we connect norms to a claim to rightness. Whereas theoretical truth presupposes a communicative society of researchers, normative rightness immediately presupposes the sounding board of a social lifeworld. Norms intervene regulatively in the communal life of subjects capable of speech and action. Normative validity means that the rules of action are intersubjectively recognized by the members of a social group.

G. H. Mead has analyzed norms in terms of expectations others have about our behavior. He calls a behavioral expectation *generalized* if every member of a social group expects all others to behave in a certain way in a given situation. S acts in conformity with a norm or S fulfills a valid norm by acting in this way if he orients his action according to the situation-specific expectations to which the members of his social group are entitled:

[I]n order that one should behave "as a member of the community" the following formal conditions must hold. *First,* one must have practical knowledge of the manner in which he is to behave, and so be able to know whether or not he is conforming. *Second,* it is implied and known by the agent that all other members of the community should have a similar practical knowledge about the manner in which they are to behave. *Third,* the agent knows that other members of the community will, as does he, believe that all others whom they take to be members of the community will have comparable knowledge. In short, we have a community in which each member is presumed to know how he is to behave and to believe that all others have knowledge comparable to his own.[8]

This formulation, by using the term "should," removes the ambiguity inherent in Mead's own formulations of the term "behavioral expectation." If we understand "behavioral expectation" in the purely cognitive sense of S_2 predicting the behavior of S_1, then the mere generalization across members of a group cannot give rise to a norm. A behavioral expectation generalized in this sense would imply, for example, that S_1 knows that S_2 expects in a given situation that S_1 will behave in a certain way. And since some other member S_n knows that S_1 knows this, S_n too will expect that S_1 will meet S_2's expectation. But then the "generalized behavioral expectation" would be just another term for "accepted theory of the everyday" (in the sense explicated by Jarvie). Yet the concept of a behavioral expectation contains not only the sense of a prediction, but also the normative sense that members of a social group are mutually *entitled* to expect certain types of behavior from one another.

One might say that theories, too, if true and applicable to certain situations, entitle one to certain expectations. However, being entitled to a conditional prediction rests on the truth of empirical statements, whereas the expectation that S will abide by a norm is justified only if *S* belongs to a social group where this norm (as expression of a general interest) is recognized. The kind of justification varies according to the type of validity claim that can be raised for a generalized behavioral expectation. When they become a component of norms, values lose their particularity in a similar way as do beliefs when they attain the status of theoretical statements. However, the universality of norms is based on the generalizability of the interests they express. It is this relation to the *Bedürfnisnatur* that emerges in the ought of a norm, but is missing in the truth or objective validity of a theory. A theory justifies the expectation that a certain event will occur if certain conditions obtain; a norm justifies the expectation that *S* will behave in a certain way in certain situations if we can assume she recognizes this norm and orients her action according to the values embodied in it.

4 Language

The sociological application of the two models of intentional and norm-governed action unproblematically presupposes language as the medium of communication, which connects subjects who act. If the rules are conceived of as semantic conventions, then the use of linguistic symbols can be elucidated by means of the concept of rule-following that I have introduced. However, this rule-model of language use is perceived from opposite perspectives, depending on whether participation in communication is represented as an intentional action or as the fulfillment of a norm. In the former case, language is conceived as the medium in which the actor expresses her beliefs and attitudes and through which she transmits the informational content of her intentions by using linguistic means to make another actor recognize what she means or intends. Language is essentially represented as a *medium for transmitting intentional experiences.*[9] In the latter case, language is understood as a medium wherein a consensus on general situation interpretations is secured among members of a social group in the light of common cultural values and norms. Sharing a common symbolic system means belonging to an intersubjectively binding form of life. Here, language is represented essentially as a *medium of participation in the same culture.* The commonality here is secured not only through using the same language, but also and foremost through recognizing the same values.

In the former case, subjects acting intentionally subsequently enter into a communicative relation with one another. Along with the normative content of the processes of reaching understanding, what is lost on this model of language is the notion of a reality constituted by the intersubjective recognition of reciprocally raised universal claims to validity. In the latter, the subjectivity of the participants is submerged in the normative consensus about the culture that is objectively given in the linguistic world view. This model of language leaves no room for any interpretive competence on the part of the individual vis-à-vis the values and norms of her lifeworld. This is the point where our critique began.

The normative model of action conceives of language as a medium wherein consensus about values becomes habitual and is reproduced. Conventional role theory, which I discuss elsewhere, is based on this assumption. Here I only want to mention that the critique of role-theory has paid particular attention to the constitutive achievements of the actor. We must not proceed from the assumption that the motives for action simply correspond to the values that are institutionalized in roles. Nor may we assume that the participant's situation interpretations and their orientations to action are guided exclusively by norms and fully congruent with roles so as to be subsumed by them. Rather, the mutual understanding attained in any particular sequence of interaction is the result of a process of reaching understanding. The participating subjects undertake this process within a context they do not fully control. Nonetheless, it is an endeavor in which they are engaged *together* in virtue of their interactive competencies. The participants coordinate their mutual expectations by orienting themselves by institutionalized values. But social roles are idealizations that serve as guidelines for constructing shared situation definitions. The process of role-taking is a context-dependent, reciprocal interpretive process aimed at reaching mutual understanding. It develops and revises an existing tradition of values and norms by means of applying and extending them as much as it is itself determined by that tradition.

Interpretation is the fundamental concept of a model of *communicative action*. The goal of such a model is to compensate for the respective weaknesses of the models of intentional and norm-governed action and to take proper account of the constitutive significance of linguistic communication. The fundamental concept of interpretation shows that the model of communicative action emphasizes the constitutive activities of participants in interaction, but does not revert to a subjectivist position. Intentional agents do not enter into communicative relations with one another after the fact, so to speak, in order to fabricate an intersubjective world. Rather, communicative action presupposes the normative reality of a society just as much as an objectifiable reality and the subjectivity of the agent herself. For every interpretation refers to a context in which these three elements are interwoven: norms and values, objects and states of affairs, and intentional experiences.

Of course the concept of interpretation easily leads to the misconception that the activity of the communicative agent is in the first instance that of a cognizing subject who first interprets a situation and then goes about disseminating that interpretation socially. This misunderstanding can be avoided by (a) tying the concept of communicative action to the condition that participating subjects assume an attitude oriented toward reaching understanding rather than toward reaching success, and (b) tying mutual understanding to a consensus not only about truth claims, but also about sincerity- and rightness claims. For then the process of interpretations that mutually refer to one another will be subject not only to the parameters of a given particular context, but to the exacting presupposition that a consensus can be attained only *by way of the shared recognition of universal validity claims*. And since rightness and sincerity belong to these validity claims as much as propositional truth does, interpretation (which, in communicative action, is conceived of as a process of mutual understanding) means the search for a mutual agreement about a situation definition. This definition refers to what is commonly recognized as the society's normative reality, what is mutually recognized as the manifested subjectivity of a participant, as well as to accepted beliefs about an objectified reality.

Reflections on Communicative Pathology (1974)

My point of departure is the assumption that the development of interactive competence regulates the construction [*Aufbau*] of internal behavioral controls. However, the systematic differences between moral judgment and the actual behavior in situations of conflict resolution show that the two lines of development do not coincide. Linguistic communication is relevant for motivational development in two respects. On the one hand, communicative action is the medium of socialization through which the influences of familial environments are filtered and transmitted to the personality system. On the other hand, language offers a way of organizing wants and needs that are subject to interpretation; our need-based nature [*Bedürfnisnatur*] is communicatively structured. The difference between levels of moral judgment and levels of moral action can be explained by disturbances of the socialization process. These "disturbances" can be analyzed on two levels: the level of pathogenetic patterns of the linguistic environment that are relevant to socialization, and the level of the structures of needs and of behavioral controls that develop under conditions of systematically distorted communication. Freud introduces the ego function of unconscious repression as a mechanism of linguistic pathogenesis. The repression of conflicts that are not consciously resolved, that is, not on a basis of consensual action, leaves traces that take the form of communicative disturbances. Intrapsychic disturbances of the communication between parts of the personality system are analogous to disturbances in family communication. Of course the analysis of such deviations presupposes knowledge [*Kenntnis*] of the kind of communication that can be characterized as "normal." But when can a communication be considered undisturbed, not systematically distorted, or "normal"?

(1) First, we have to explain the sense in which we mean to talk about the normalcy conditions of linguistic communication. Obviously, the *statistical notion* of normalcy is unsuitable. A normal distribution of communicative features tells us nothing about the normalcy conditions of socially effective interactions, unless we have already classified the populations being examined based on clinical criteria; but that would be to evaluate them based on criteria of normalcy. Otherwise we could not rule out an "abnormal" scenario,

whether the deviating individuals or linguistic units it comprised were greater or fewer in number than average. The *clinical notion* of normalcy stems from the field of somatic illnesses. Here, the healthy or normative state [*Sollzustand*] of the organism, from which the state of illness deviates, is reasonably well known. That is, we either know it through empirical analysis or by means of intuitively interpreted empirical indicators. Transferring this notion of normalcy to the realm of psychic or communicative disturbances is difficult because the currently available theories have not been able to determine unequivocally the norms [*Sollwerte*] of psychic organization. Any proposals that appeal to intuitive evidence are suspect of deriving from cultural traditions that are not made explicit. Nowadays, therefore, the *culturalistic notion* of normalcy characterizes a widely accepted fallback position. According to this notion, we have to confine ourselves to a descriptive account of what a given culture considers to be "normal" for a given domain of life. Thus the key to the culturally relative concepts of normalcy is not the normal distribution of observed aspects of behavior, but the definitions of normalcy that are to be ascertained in any given case.

However, ethnopsychiatry has raised strong reservations regarding this relativism that is widely accepted in cultural anthropology. G. Devereux[1] suggests some distinctions that clearly show the limits of the argument for cultural relativism. He juxtaposes individual pathologies with disturbances that have been culturally standardized, and shows that even these disturbances, which have been normalized, as it were, deviate from what is normal in the clinical sense. Cultural normalization refers to all three elements of the "disturbance":[2]

(i) the interpretation of the disturbing or shocking events that are experienced as stress or trauma and trigger an intrapsychic conflict (in Sparta, a mother's mourning a son who has died in battle is an "ethnic disturbance," because its cause is a culturally recognized and conventionalized trauma, whereas in Athens, the same act of mourning remains at the level of an individual emotional reaction);

(ii) strategies of repression whereby the intrapsychic conflict can be kept out of consciousness and made bearable (i.e., not therapeutically "resolved"). Every culture, even in cases of extreme disturbance (as Devereux's elaborate example of the shaman demonstrates), offers a system of preferences for means of repression that allow for a superficial normalization (i.e., a conventionally recognized restructuring) of the inner conflict;

(iii) finally, the symptoms in which the unconsciously repressed conflict may be manifested. (Under this heading Devereux examines social roles that institutionalize culturally recognized deviant behavior: that of the shaman, the person run amok, the "mad dog," the Mohave transvestite, the stoic saint, etc. Even where such roles have not been differentiated, there are cultural definitions for "how to behave when one is crazy.")

Individual disturbances occur to the extent that the normalizing activity of a culture fails in such a way that the person affected has to improvise for herself how to interpret traumatic events and which means of repression and types of symptoms to choose. Perhaps a comparative concept formation is preferable to the dichotomous concept formation that juxtaposes ethnic and individual disturbances and leads to the postulation of an "ethnic unconscious." But even if Devereux's thesis is weakened in this sense and disturbances are classified according to their degree of cultural *stereotyping*, the analysis of limit cases is of critical importance for the culturalistic notion of normalcy.

The cross-cultural comparison of ethnopsychiatric phenomena shows that the conventional restructuring of forms of repression and of symptoms normalizes the underlying anomaly of a serious psychic conflict or illness in the sense of socially accepted roles. However, it does so in such a way that the anomaly remains perceptible as such. The shaman is psychologically ill in the clinical sense even though he plays a socially recognized role:

The primitive who, after suffering from psychological disturbances, undergoes a shamanic treatment that "cures" him and makes him a shaman, in reality only experiences a conventional restructuring of his conflicts and symptoms without thereby gaining any *real insight* into the nature of his conflicts. . . . These cures take place as if the treatment consisted merely in replacing conflicts and cultural repression by conventional cultural conflicts and ritualized symptoms, without ever producing the insight which alone can lead to a real cure.[3]

Devereux tells of two Native American Indians sentenced to death, who had been deemed "of sound mind in the legal sense" by the prison psychiatrist because they took their hallucinations from the cultural material of the beliefs of their tribe. Only a closer examination showed that they no longer objectively lived these cultural contents, but used them for hallucinatory purposes.[4] The psychiatrist had confused the hallucinations of his patients with the beliefs of the tribe of which they were members. Similarly, the difference between delirium and faith can also be rendered culturally inconspicuous if the person affected "clothes" his clinical behavior in a social role, say that of the shaman, and normalizes it. Hence the psychiatrist assessing psychic disturbances according to a cultural notion of normalcy is

incapable of helping an Indian who is in remission after a first psychotic attack or urge and defines himself as a shaman. According to "relativistic" norms that govern the limited diagnostic technique I am talking about, one would claim that this Indian shaman has no need of psychiatric treatment, since he can be considered "culturally normal." However, I have shown that the shaman is either a severe neurotic or a psychotic in remission and hence is in urgent need of psychiatric aid. In fact, such an individual is in remission *only* with respect to *a single* socially determined milieu: his own tribe. He is more or less well adapted to this, and *only* this, milieu. *He is not capable of adapting, and especially not capable of re-adapting.* A normal Indian, in contrast, who is not a shaman, can be well adapted to his culture and still retain his ability to cope with a variety of situations. In my opinion, the touchstone of mental health is not adaptedness as such, but a subject's ability to develop *further* through successive *new* adaptations without losing the sense of his own temporal continuity.[5]

Devereux pursues the normalizing activities of culture somewhat further than proponents of cultural relativism do. He shows that disturbances and deviations themselves are subject to the definitions of normalcy, albeit only in such a way that the difference between normal and deviant behavior is simply leveled out rather than made unrecognizable.

The distinction drawn here requires a culturally invariant notion of normalcy. It must be corroborated by clinical experience, but explicated independently. In the last passage quoted above, Devereux cites as the determining criterion the ability to restructure one's own identity in accordance with one's situation. Elsewhere, he thinks that all psychological disturbances result in dedifferentiation and deindividuation.[6] Yet "individuation" is a concept laden with presuppositions, and the concept of a level of differentiation is useful only if we can give an adequate characterization of the appropriate system—precisely by means of the dynamic of progressive individuation.

The cultural concept of normalcy turns out to be untenable. Yet a culturally invariant concept of normalcy that refers neither to features of physical health nor to statistical averages has a normative content. How can this content be justified within an empirical-descriptive science?

Piaget used the concept of developmental logic, which permits the introduction of normative notions for purposes of empirical analysis. The concept has so far been corroborated only in the domain of *cognitive development*. Here, the normative assumption [*Wertprämisse*] is not suspect, for the development of objectifying thought is measured by the level of unequivocally decidable problems, that is, of problems that have *true solutions*. Propositional truth is a validity claim presupposed by any argumentation. *Normative rightness* of action and evaluation is a validity claim that is under dispute, but can still be made plausible. Research into the developmental logic of moral judgment depends on this normative assumption. Its ontogenesis is also measured according to levels of problem solving. But in this case we cannot rely on elementary knowledge of logic, mathematics, and physics for validating the correct solutions. We have to venture onto the unstable ground of philosophical ethics in order to justify the thesis that each higher level of moral consciousness allows for an increasingly adequate consensual solution of increasingly complex conflicts of action. Expanding the concept of the capacity for moral judgment into the concept of interactive competence once again transforms the normative assumption. For the ability to participate in interaction and to maintain the consensual basis of communicative action even through conflicts includes the competence to act in accordance with moral judgments, but, beyond this, also presupposes the validity basis of linguistic communication *in its full spectrum*. Interactive competence is measured not according to the ability to solve problems of knowledge and moral insight at the appropriate level, but according to the ability to maintain processes of reaching mutual understanding even in conflict situations rather than breaking off communication or merely seeming to maintain it.

The psychoanalytic concept of unconscious repression sheds light, as we shall see, on the technique of apparently carrying on processes of reaching consensual understanding. Unconsciously repressed conflicts arise—either intrapsychically as an interruption of communication within the self, or as an inconspicuous barrier between individuals within the family—under conditions that exclude processes of mutual understanding and hence healing (conflict resolution) through insight. The concept of normalcy for ego strength developed by psychoanalysis in this connection is measured by the dependence on strategies of unconscious repression. The ego's strength increases to the same extent that the ego is able to do without such strategies and to process its conflicts consciously. The normative assumption here lies in the concept of *consciousness* and in the relation to the *insight* into an interpersonally caused psychological conflict. In accordance with my communication-theoretic reading of the basic psychoanalytic assumptions,[7] I relate these topologically conceived conditions of conscious conflict processing to conditions of normal linguistic communication: Conscious conflict processing means conflict processing under conditions of undistorted communication.

Thus we return to where we began our reflections, having found that we cannot avail ourselves of the available statistical, clinical, or cultural notions of normalcy that are at our disposal. Rather we have to make explicit the normative content inherent in the notion of linguistic communication itself. The expression "undistorted communication" does not add anything to mutual linguistic understanding [*Verständigung*], for "mutual understanding" signifies the telos inherent in linguistic communication. I would like to establish the conditions of normalcy of linguistic communication by way of a conceptual analysis of the meaning of "mutual understanding" because I assume that every speech act has an unavoidable, as it were, transcendentally necessitating basis of validity. I want to develop the thesis that every communicative actor has to commit to fulfilling universal claims to validity. Insofar as she participates in communication (i.e., a process of reaching understanding) at all, she cannot avoid raising the following claims:

(i)   to *express* herself intelligibly,

(ii) to make *something* understood,

(iii) to make *herself* understood in doing so, and

(iv) to reach a mutual understanding *with another.*

Of course if complete agreement [*Einverständnis*], which encompasses all four components, were the normal state of linguistic communication, then it would not be necessary to analyze the process of reaching mutual understanding under the dynamic aspect of *bringing about* agreement. What is typical instead are situations that lie in the gray area somewhere between a lack of understanding [*Unverständnis*] and misunderstanding [*Missverständnis*], intended and involuntary insincerity, veiled and open disagreement on the one hand, and an always already existing pre-understanding [*Vorverständigtsein*] and mutual understanding on the other. In this gray area, agreement must be actively brought about. Mutual understanding is a process that seeks to overcome a lack of understanding and misunderstanding, insincerity toward oneself and others, and disagreement. And it does so on the common basis of validity claims that aim at reciprocal recognition.

I would now like to consider the ontogenesis of the validity basis (2) in order to then demonstrate the transcendental import of the claims that ground validity and that precede every possible instance of communication (3). Starting from this validity basis and the general structures of linguistic communication, I shall then discuss formal conditions of systematically distorted communication (4). Finally, I shall discuss a few examples of such communication.

(2) Having studied prelinguistic child development, R. Spitz[8] attributes particular importance to learning processes in the third month of life whereby primary narcissism is overcome and the stage of the first "object anticipation" sets in. From the perspective of the constituents of linguistic communication, the following three moments seem significant: (a) The child learns to distinguish sounds that it produces itself from external acoustic stimuli (babbling monologues) and it begins to react with understanding [*Verständnis*] to the physiognomic schema of the mother's face (smiling with eye contact). (b) The child learns to act in a goal-directed fashion based on schemata of sensory-motor action. Along with these beginnings of initiatives to act, we can observe (c) a transformation from reactions to stimuli to proto-forms of intentional action guided by perception. From the very beginning, the actions serve the double task of controlling the environment and of fending off danger. In doing this they regulate drives and affects. This third aspect sheds light on the beginnings of the communicative structuring of inner nature. The first two aspects refer to the development of communicative relations and the corresponding capabilities of active and passive participants in interaction.

In the second half of the first year of life, the love object "mother" is constituted for the child as an identifiable entity. First, the child learns to integrate into a single image two object anticipations: the "good," permissive mother and the "bad," restrictive or absent one. This synthesis marks equally a cognitive development (the beginnings of object permanence) and an increasing regulation of affects and drives (beginnings of the tolerance for ambivalence). The *eighth-month anxiety* that then follows (and which Spitz analyzes in detail) signals that the child learns to distinguish between the trusted and loved object of the mother and strangers. The child no longer reacts only with understanding to the physiognomic schema (be it that of the mother, a mask, or a stranger). Rather he now responds to the gestures of an individual reference person. This alters the level of relations between partners in communication. The child identifies with the mother by imitating her gestures. This is an important precondition for the exchange, mediated through gestures, whereby the child learns to regulate his own activity in relation to that of the mother (i.e., giving and taking, being active and passive). For this self-regulation of the initiative to act, shaking one's head in denial plays a significant role.

First the child learns the gesture of shaking his head by identifying with the mother who refuses him something by shaking her head. Later, the child uses the negating shaking of the head in situations where he *rejects* a demand or offer *himself*. And after language development has begun with the first holophrastic (one-word) sentences, from approximately the fifteenth month, the child uses the word "no" instead of the negating gesture. This step is the beginning of linguistic communication in a specificc

With the acquisition of the gesture of negation, action is replaced by word, and communication across distance is introduced. This may be the most important turning point in the development of the individual and the species. This is the beginning of the humanization of the species, of the *zoon politikon*, of society.[9]

Spitz, I think rightly, attributes a crucial importance to the gesture of denial on the part of the prelinguistic child and to the nay-saying of the child who has only just begun to speak in the transition from *symbolically mediated* to genuinely linguistic communication. Yet the insistence with which he does so does not fit well with the analytic conception of this phenomenon. Spitz speaks of the conceptual character of negation. He believes that negation makes possible the capacity to judge [*Urteilsfähigkeit*]. But the first "no" is neither the negation [*Verneinung*] of predicates ("this ball is not red"), nor the negation [*Negation*] of states of affairs ("it is not true that this ball is red"). Otherwise the child would already be able to distinguish different types of speech acts or interpersonal relations. The first "no" is rather constitutive for producing symbolically mediated interpersonal relations tout court. It makes possible that early mode of the first linguistic communication which is, in a way, determined by imperatives.

In prelinguistic interactions with a reference person, the child experiences satisfactions as well as frustrations, but the frustrations of drives are in the first instance externally imposed events; they are not yet perceived *as prohibitions*. Only after the child has learned, through a process of identification, to understand the refusals the mother imposes on him as intentional actions and has himself learned to say no, does he meet the precondition for participating in a communicative relationship for which the option of obeying or accepting and refusing is constitutive. A request is not a request, an offer not an offer, as long as the addressee lacks the conscious ability to say no, that is, the ability, in principle, to decide not to abide by the request or to accept the offer. The first "no" negates an expectation of behavior. To say no means rejection. Spitz describes the psycho-dynamics of this first nay-saying that is constitutive for the interpersonal relationship between speakers as follows:

The negating gesture of shaking one's head and the word "no" uttered by the Object are incorporated [*einverleibt*] into the ego of the infant as memory traces. The negative affect is separated from this representation. This separation triggers a frustration that is then linked through association with the memory trace in the ego. If the child identifies with the Object, this identification with the attacker is followed by an attack on the outside world, according to Anna Freud. For the fifteen-month-old child, this concept takes the form of "no" (first the gesture, then the word). The child has adopted this form of the concept from its love object. Based on numerous experiences of displeasure, the "no" carries a negative valence. As a result, "no" is suitable for expressing aggression, and this is why "no" is used in the defense mechanism of identifying with the attacker and turned against the Object. As soon as this level is reached, the phase of defiance (the well-known "terrible twos") can begin.[10]

Saying "no" is not significant in language development simply because the child performs her first speech act with the first intentional "no." Rather, saying "no" is a central indicator of language development because the child is only able to perform a speech act, that is, to enter into a linguistically mediated interpersonal relation, once she understands orders, prohibitions, or offers as requests that can be denied, that is, as behavioral expectations that can be negated. On this *first level of linguistic communication,* concepts, which have developed prelinguistically and have hitherto structured the interactive realm, can be restructured:

(i) There is a differentiation between primitive linguistic expressions and nonlinguistic gestures and actions. *Communicative symbols* express behavioral expectations and thus remain rooted in a context of action, whereas nonlinguistic actions are connected to linguistically produced *interpersonal relations* as the fulfillment or nonfulfillment of behavioral expectations.

(ii) The *semantic content* communicated by means of symbols and actions represents a syndrome in which certain meanings of the imperative mode of communication (requests, offers) are fused with propositional contents (in reference to objects in the world) and certain intentions of the speaker (sympathy, antipathy, pleasure, pain, etc.).

(iii) The concepts of the *actor* and of *agency* are determined by the *complementary relation* between the behavioral expectation that the alter expresses by means of a communicative symbol and the action whereby the ego fulfills or thwarts this expectation. Interlocutors act from *reciprocal perspectives*—under conditions of a double contingency: For both, it is possible in principle to frustrate the expectations of the other.

(iv) Although the imperative mode of communication does not yet admit of any alternative uses of language, it does establish an immediate connection between *communication* and *the regulation of behavior.* By performing a speech act, one individual influences the motives of the other. Since linguistically produced interpersonal relations presuppose in principle the possibility of rejection, *motives for action* must be constrained to compensate for this new degree of freedom.

(v) Inasmuch as interactions are embedded in power relations, behavioral expectations can be sanctioned on the basis of symbolically generalized pleasure/pain. That is, they can be enforced by means of the prospect of *rewards* and the threat of punishment. Through this mechanism, drives and affects are transformed into motives for action. The prelinguistic predispositions of one's inner nature are drawn into an intersubjectively shared universe through communicative action, and this is how culturally interpreted needs are created.

The development of the *second level of communication* can be examined from the perspective of the differentiation of language as a peculiar domain of reality. The linguistic utterance is differentiated from (a) other semantically contentful, but nonverbal expressions (gestures); (b) the context of action in which it is embedded; (c) normative social reality (norms of action and values); (d) the subjectivity of the speakers; and (e) the community of those participating in communication. All these relations manifest themselves in (f) the internal organization of speech; they determine the validity basis of linguistic communication. The reference point of the following rough developmental sketch is a level of interaction that presupposes propositionally differentiated speech.

(a) A grammatical speech act is distinct from nonverbal acts and gestures, that is, bodily expressions, on the one hand, and from symbolic but not propositionally differentiated forms of representation such as music, dance, painting, and so on, on the other.

Speech acts and nonverbal expressions can be functional equivalents of one another. Hailing a cab nonverbally can be replaced with a verbalized call. Silently taking someone's arm can, in the appropriate context, *mean* the same as the assurance "I'll help you." In still other cases, there is a complementary relationship between categories of expressions. A verbal promise can be kept by nonverbal actions. These actions then have the *meaning* that the speaker "has kept his word." Linguistic and nonlinguistic expressions can express the same speaker intention, and the semantic content of both types of expression can by analyzed from the dual perspective of the interpersonal relation and the propositional content. There remains, to be sure, the difference that speech acts become reflexive, that is, they can be turned into the reference point or content of other speech acts.

The linguistic and nonlinguistic means whereby communicative acts are performed stand on the same level of organization, so to speak. This is not the case for speech acts and gestures. For bodily expressions are not related to the psychological process they express conventionally in the way that sentential symbols are to their semantic content. They are often the sign *(index)* as well as the icon of what they mean. Bühler has sought to capture this difference between the gestural and linguistic functions of meaning with the concepts of expressive versus representative function; Bateson with the distinction, borrowed from computer science, between analog and digital transmission; and Arieti with the juxtaposition of proto-language and normal language, a juxtaposition geared toward psychopathological phenomena. What defines these conceptualizations is the view that propositions contain general predicates. These must be connected to individual objects through acts of identification, whereas the

meaning of a gesture is explicated by its own concrete visual character and is from the outset rooted in the context in which it is expressed so that an explicit reference is unnecessary.

The bodily expression is unencumbered by problems of reference
and by decisions about the context-specific application and
concretization of *general* terms because it lacks a propositionally articulated structure.

(b) A further aspect of this development is the transition from
context-dependent language use in symbolically mediated interactions to *context-independent language use* in propositionally differentiated speech. As long as the dominant mode of communication is
uniformly structured by imperatives and does not allow for differentiated language use, speech acts remain rooted in the context of action inasmuch as the situation *in* which an utterance is made
coincides with the situation *to* which its content refers. But as soon as
propositional content can be kept invariant with respect to different
illocutionary acts and correspondingly changing interpersonal relations, sentence meaning has to be reconnected to the speech situation by means of expressions that *refer* to the situation and belong to
the system of reference that has now emerged. The flip side of freeing propositional content from the imperative web of interactions, of
which the utterance itself is a part, is the above-mentioned problem
of reference and application. Names or definite descriptions have to
be chosen by the speaker in such a way that a hearer in a given situation could reliably identify the object to which the expression refers,
that is, that she could pick it out from a number of possible objects of
reference.

The developments discussed under (a) and (b) create a new level
of linguistic differentiation. Insofar as a speaker remains below this
level, his utterances take on *idiosyncratic features*. Both inconsistencies
between verbalized semantic content and content expressed in nonverbal actions or gestures, as well as the arbitrary application of public language with opaque references betray a deformed language use
that is shot through with *private meanings*.

(c), (d) A further tendency toward the increasing autonomy of
language emerges in the separation of speech from the normative

background of speech acts. Elsewhere, I have shown that the systematic connection of participant and observer perspective is constitutive for roles, that is, for reciprocal normative behavioral expectations. This splits the domain of the reality of symbolically mediated interactions in two: Norms of action and values form the relatively invariant background against which interpretive events take place in sequences of speech acts, nonverbal actions, and gestures. This differentiation between speech and normative social reality corresponds to the differentiation between speech and a speaker's subjectivity. The double-sided differentiation of speech from the institutional reality of norms of action and values as well as from the symbolically organized ego of agents who take their place within systems of roles leads to a greater complexity in processes of reaching understanding. At the level of symbolically mediated interaction, reaching understanding within the mode of imperative communication means both getting the other to understand a behavioral expectation and to fulfill it. "Reaching understanding" [*Verständigung*] today still has the above-mentioned dual connotation of understanding [*Verstehen*] and agreeing [*Übereinstimmen*]. As soon as speech is detached from its normative background and from the identity of the speaker, the shared understanding [*Verständnis*] of the meaning [*Sinn*] of an expression in itself no longer guarantees agreement about its rightness and acceptability. In such a case, dissensus regarding the rightness of an utterance that is intelligible in terms of its semantic content may concern the fact that the utterance (i) fails to meet a commonly recognized norm or (ii) accords with a disputed norm. The dissensus, however, may also refer to the self-representation of the speaker, that is, to the fact (iii) that an utterance does not fit with a recognized identity or an ego-ideal or (iv) that it accords with an identity that is itself contested.

(e) Speech becomes autonomous relative to other forms of expression, relative to the context of action, relative to normative social reality and the speaker's subjectivity. The result is that speech becomes subject to *an external organization* that resolves the steering problems that crop up. Socially, for example, there are questions as to who may participate (actively or passively) in which speech situations, how formally or diffusely relationships get defined, and so on.

Temporally, there are issues regarding who may start or stop discussion, who may contribute something to the conversation, how often, and in what order. In terms of content, there are issues regarding the order of topics and contributions, how precisely topics are defined and how extensively they get treated, how broad the spectrum of contributions should be, and so on. Of course the normative context that determines the patterns of interaction is also represented in the external organization of speech. But in addition, speech is subject to its own organizing imperatives. Moreover, it serves as the arena where speakers have to reconcile different institutional contexts and coordinate their differential plans of action and their needs. Thus each participant can try to influence the external organization of speech with the aim of altering the normative context to her advantage. The autonomy of speech opens up the possibility of employing the *means of communicative action strategically* without ostensibly violating the commitment to consensus. Some examples of this are debates over the order of business in associations and parliaments, conversations in informal groups, and especially habitual speech strategies in the family that serve the undeclared pursuit of unapproved interests under the presupposition of consensual action (and consensual conflict resolution). Egocentric perspectives may be built into the asymmetries of how speech is organized in more or less obvious ways.

(f) The differentiation of speech that I have elaborated under (a) through (e) is mirrored by the *internal organization of speech*. The external organization of speech normatively determines (i.e., through regulations of an institutional nature) how the general steering problems of a linguistic system of communication are resolved. The internal organization of speech consists in the universal pragmatic regulation of sequences of speech acts, and this regulation does not require any backing by social norms owing to its transcendentally necessitating nature.

As the independent sphere of grammatical structures that are formed in accordance to (or violation of) certain rules described under (a) becomes autonomous, the need arises for evaluating an utterance as an element of a language. An utterance is *unintelligible* if it does not belong to the set of well-formed expressions that can be produced by means of the appropriate system of grammatical rules. The differentiation of propositional contents described under (b) gives rise to the need to judge whether a proposition is *true* or *false,* and whether an object of which something is asserted can be identified or not, that is, whether the proposition could be true or whether it is *meaningless.* The separation between speech and a normative background indicated in (c) gives rise to the need to judge a given utterance with respect to whether it meets socially binding values or a prevailing norm and is in that sense *right* or whether it violates established structures of expectation. Similarly, the split between speech and a speaker's subjectivity cited under (d) raises the need to judge the speaker's expressed intention with regard to whether the speaker expresses it *sincerely* or *insincerely.*

In performing speech acts, we are required to meet universal demands that ground the validity of our claims. These demands reflect the relationships between the speech acts and their proper linguistic medium, the normative social reality, and the inner subjective nature of the speakers. As soon as this validity basis of speech is established, different modes of language use can be differentiated depending on which validity claim is thematically highlighted: There are cognitive, interactive, and expressive uses of language. The occurrence of these different modes of communication is a necessary condition for performative negation, that is, for extending the negation of sentences to speech acts. At the first level of communication only the behavioral expectation of another can be negated; at the second level, the speaker is able to distinguish between a rejection of what is proposed in the speech act (I don't accept your promise), a negated speech act (I am not promising you that I will come), and a negated proposition (I promise that I will not come).

(3) In discussing the "transcendental" place value of the validity basis, one might think that it is impossible to diverge from the universal demands that ground validity, that the internal organization of speech is inviolable. If that were the case, we would not even need to explicate the normative foundation of speech since the normal conditions of communication from which a speaker could not diverge would be of no interest for analyzing distorted patterns of communication. On the other hand, normalcy conditions for the external organization of speech seem to be given in a different sense than the conditions for its internal organization. The problems regarding temporal, spatial, and substantive dispositions leave considerable leeway for standardization, which can be utilized differently depending on the functional context in which communication takes place. The key to the pathogenesis of linguistic communication, in my view, lies in a certain *overburdening of the external organization of speech*. This burden *must be shifted onto the internal organization of speech* and results in systematic distortion. I use the term "distortion" to stress the insight that the internal organization of speech expresses universal and unavoidable presuppositions of linguistic communication. The transcendental necessity implied by this feature of ineluctability or of a lack of alternatives does not imply inviolability. Rather, it means that the violation of the internal organization of speech gives rise to pathological mutations of the patterns of communication. In other words, the pathogenesis can be traced back to problems that exert pressure on the external organization of speech. When this pressure is shifted from the external to the internal organization of speech, it has a distorting effect. I should now like to analyze this distortion, which *sets in at the validity basis of speech*.

The disturbance of systematically distorted communication lies at a deeper level than the disturbance of anomalous behavior that expresses itself in divergence from a socially binding norm. Distorted communication does not violate any norms of action that enjoy social validity for contingent reasons; they violate universal presuppositions of communication that in no way change from one normative context to another. Of course even a flawed communication is a communication, which in many cases may still be regarded as normal speech—"normal" in the cultural sense of normalcy that covers everything within the bounds of what is socially accepted.

The following are *universal presuppositions of communicative action:*

(i) that the participants mutually consider each other to be *accountable*. That is, they must presume one another to have overcome childish egocentrism and to be able to distinguish between the intersubjectivity of language, the objectivity of external nature, the subjectivity of inner nature, and the normativity of society; and

Reflections on Communicative Pathology

(ii) that they mutually consider one another *ready and willing to reach mutual understanding*. They must mutually suppose one another to be disposed either to act on the basis of or to bring about a consensus regarding the four validity claims inherent in speech (the intelligibility of an utterance, the truth of the asserted or mentioned propositional content, the rightness of the utterance with reference to an accepted normative background, and the sincerity of the speaker regarding the intentions she is expressing). In other words, they must attribute to each other dispositions to *reach agreement*. This general communicative presupposition of a mutually attributed willingness to reach mutual understanding does not hold for strategic, but only for communicative action. Thus a speaker S who is willing to reach mutual understanding will

(a) select a linguistic expression so that the hearer H understands it as S intends H to understand it;

(b) formulate the propositional content so that it represents an experience or a fact (and so that H can share S's knowledge);

(c) express her intention so that the linguistic expression represents what S means (and so that H may trust S);

(d) execute the speech act so that it meets accepted norms or corresponds to accepted self-images (and so that H can agree with S on this).

The validity of the *sentence* used depends on whether it is *well formed* in accordance with grammatical rules. The validity of the *proposition* (or the existential presuppositions of a propositional content) depends on whether it (or they) *correspond(s)* to reality. The validity of the *intention* expressed depends on whether it *coincides* with what the speaker means. And, finally, the validity of the speech act depends on whether it *fulfills* acknowledged background norms.

If the *intelligibility* of a communication breaks down, the communicative disturbance can be thematized at the level of hermeneutic discourse, in connection with the relevant linguistic system. In cognitive language use, we take on an obligation to ground our claim [*Begründungsverpflichtung*] that is inherent in the speech act. Constative speech acts contain the offer to take recourse, if necessary, to the experiential source from which the speaker draws the certainty that his statement is true. If this immediate grounding [*Begründung*] fails to satisfy an ad hoc doubt, the problematized truth claim can become the object of a theoretical discourse. In interactive language use, we take on an obligation to justify our claim [*Rechtfertigungsverpflichtung*] inherent in the speech act. Regulative speech acts contain only the offer of a speaker to refer, if necessary, to the normative context that gives the speaker the *conviction* that her utterance is right. Once again, if the immediate justification [*Rechtfertigung*] fails to remove an ad hoc doubt, we may move to the level of discourse, in this case of practical discourse. With this move, however, the object of the discursive test becomes not the claim to normative validity that is connected to the speech act; but the *validity claim of the underlying norm.* Lastly, even in expressive language use, the speaker undertakes a warrant inherent in the speech act, namely, the obligation to prove trustworthy [*Bewährungsverpflichtung*] by demonstrating through the consequences of his actions that he has expressed the intention that actually motivates him. In case the immediate *assurance* that expresses what is *evident* to the speaker himself fails to dissipate an ad hoc doubt, the sincerity of the utterance can only be tested against the consistency of the consequences of action.

Now what does a violation of the universal presuppositions of communication mean?

An utterance must be sufficiently well formed so that it can be understood. Otherwise it does not serve the purpose of reaching mutual understanding. It is not possible to want to communicate *and* to express oneself unintelligibly or misleadingly: herein lies the necessitating moment that is reminiscent of a transcendental necessity. Intelligibility is a claim that can be satisfied to a degree: An utterance may be more or less intelligible, but it must be intelligible *überhaupt* (i.e., sufficiently so) if it is to fulfill its communicative purpose. It is possible to set different standards of intelligibility for utterances depending on their particular functional contexts. For example, the standards of precision and demands for explication in science are different from those of everyday communication. I would like to compare several violations of the claim to intelligibility in order to identify the conditions under which something like a systematic distortion of communication occurs.

(a) A speaker wishes to express himself in a foreign language of which he has limited mastery, but the attempt fails. His utterances remain unintelligible. Yet the speaker would be perfectly able to express what he means intelligibly in his mother tongue. I do not call this a case of systematically distorted communication, but of incompetence. The speaker is incompetent to express what he means within the conventions of a foreign language.

(b) A scientist fails to express herself sufficiently clearly. She abides neither by the demands for explication nor by the terminology of a discourse, which is regulated by an academic discipline. Her colleagues complain that she is unintelligible. This does not mean that her factual assertions are not intelligible, but only that they violate the norms of a level of intelligibility to be expected in the context of a specialized public sphere. In this case, communication is not distorted either.

(c) In an embarrassing situation, one of the people involved tries to express himself so as to maintain a misunderstanding that defuses the situation. This misunderstanding may have been intended or it may have arisen by accident. Or a speaker tries to express herself unintelligibly in a communicative situation that has derailed and in which any of the possible reactions would be equally embarrassing. She chooses a mild form of breaking off communication or of obfuscation in order to avoid the otherwise unavoidable conflict. Neither is so much a case of systematically distorted communication as an instance of strategic action replacing consensual action. Intended misunderstandings and intended lack of understanding are part of a strategy in the course of which the speaker silently suspends essential presuppositions of communication (sincerity, rightness).

(d) A speaker expresses himself (in his mother tongue) unintelligibly or confusedly without noticing or intending it. The anomaly of his manner of expression may be caused by illogical or paradoxical language use. That is, verbal and nonverbal messages may contradict each other. A bizarre form of expression, however, may also result from an idiosyncratic use of semantics or from violations of syntax. If interjections of private language violate the communicative presupposition of intelligibility, and thus the internal organization of speech, even though the speaker does not intentionally abandon the foundation of consensual action, then we have what I want to call systematically distorted communication.

Something similar applies to two other validity claims: sincerity and normative rightness. Unless an intention is expressed sincerely, the speaker's intention cannot serve the purpose of reaching mutual understanding. Again, transcendental necessitation is evident in the fact that one cannot want both to make oneself understood and to express one's intention insincerely. In cognitive language use (I assert that p) the implicit intention of the speaker (that the speaker *knows* something) is not thematized. Similarly, in interactive language use (I order you that p), the speaker's embedded intentional experiences (that she gives the order fearfully, threateningly, cold-bloodedly, embarrassedly, etc.) are expressed only incidentally. Only in expressive language use (I suspect that p; I hope that p; I do not deny that I miss you, that I hate you, love you, etc.) do intentional experiences lose their secondary character. Although there is the possibility that the speaker expresses her intention sincerely or insincerely, the claim to sincerity may also be redeemed *by degree*. How much a speaker conceals behind his explicit sincere utterances depends on the context. In different functional contexts, this circumstance is grounds for standardizing the scope of sincere utterances. Examples are utterances under oath during trials or marriage ceremonies, which institutionalize a uni- or bilateral claim to "the whole truth," thus excluding strategic withholding of information. Consider the following examples:

(a) A witness is under suspicion of having given false testimony. He repeats his testimony under oath. Later it turns out that he has purposely suppressed a relevant fact without having committed an outright lie. Here the witness is violating a norm that is important to the functioning of court proceedings; namely, telling the truth to its full extent. He is acting strategically in a domain of action for which a valid norm prescribes acting on the basis of consensus.

(b) One partner in a couple pretends to have feelings that the other expects. Let's assume we are talking about a woman who does not want to endanger the normative context of the marriage and the family. For the sake of this strategic goal, she keeps up the appearance of reciprocating the affection of her husband whom she has long detested. This gives rise to two levels of communication. At the level of manifest behavior, the communicative presuppositions of consensual action are met. At the level of latent behavior, one of the participants is acting strategically and intentionally violates the presupposition of sincerity. The internal organization of speech is being unilaterally and intentionally violated.

(c) We may modify this example. The wife deceives not only her husband regarding her true feelings, but also herself. (We need not consider the structurally analogous case in which both partners relate to each other as well as to themselves insincerely, since it differs from the simple case only in degree of complexity.) Again, communication is split and transpires at the manifest level such that the conditions of communicative action are met, while at the latent level, one of the participants is acting strategically by suspending the sincerity claim. But now the speaker violates a communicative presupposition unintentionally and in such a way that the violation of the organization of speech goes unnoticed by *both parties*. In cases (b) and (c) the communication between participants is systematically distorted, but only in the latter case can the disturbance be traced back to a disruption of communication within the psyche of one of the participants.

Suspending the claim to normative rightness has similar consequences. An utterance has to fit into the normative context; otherwise it is not recognized and fails to serve the purpose of reaching mutual understanding. A transcendental necessitation asserts itself in the fact that one may not at the same time want mutual understanding and make utterances that violate recognized norms and values. Here I want to leave it open whether the normative background is equally binding for all participants or whether it mediates by means of a normative self-image and determines how *a particular person* ought to act in a given situation. I want to distinguish between the *degree of formalization* whereby a behavior is standardized and the *degree of fulfillment* of an existing norm by a particular behavior. In our context, only this deviation from norms, which cannot be further standardized, is of interest. Consider the following examples.

(a) A speaker behaves too informally by ignoring social distance and trying to create an intimacy that is inappropriate in the situation at hand. This kind of norm violation has nothing to do with distorted communication.

(b) A speaker may behave awkwardly and may not feel up to handling a particularly formal situation, such as a reception, a test, etc. Or she behaves inappropriately because she does not know what the normative context is. This is a case of behavior that deviates from the norms owing to incompetence. Again, it has nothing to do with distorted communication.

(c) Both of these are quite different from inflexible behavior that stereotypically recurs, but is not necessarily experienced by the actor as abnormal. This category includes neurotic behavior patterns— utterances that are forcibly standardized and are felt to be peculiar and out of place by others. Again, a split of communication can be observed: This time, only the speaker takes the communicative presuppositions to be met, while other participants regard the communication as flawed. The internal organization of speech is damaged at the level of manifestation; only for the speaker does the semblance of a smooth flow of communication persist.

(d) If participants disagree about the normative background, if the other considers certain norms of action to be right that the ego rejects, or if the other does not accept the ego's image of herself, then we can no longer talk about deviating behavior; instead, we now have a conflict. This can give rise to distortion effects for the internal organization of speech if the conflict is repressed and disguised and continues to smolder under the cover of apparently consensual action. Here, too, there is a split of communication, which we shall examine in detail.

I have not discussed violations of the claim to truth. The social standardization of what counts as vindicating this claim can apply only to the warrant to ground the claim, which is immanent in the speech act. I do not take on the same warrant for an assertion I make in the course of small talk as I do for a statement I make in the course of a scientific discussion. Curiously, there is no violation of truth that is symptomatic of systematically distorted communication.

(a) One can be mistaken, and one *may* be mistaken. An unintentionally false statement does not fall into the class of actions for which we are accountable. The care with which a speaker makes good on the warrant he takes on with a constative speech act can be sanctioned much like lying, but error cannot. Indeed discovering mistakes is a condition for learning. Mistakes do not affect the internal organization of speech.

(b) Things are somewhat different in the case of "wanton assertions." If by that we mean utterances in which the speaker carelessly or intentionally neglects the minimal obligations of a constative speech act, we are not dealing with assertions or at least not with correctly formed acceptable speech acts. In certain contexts, we may be dealing with assertions with which the speaker tries to make things easy for himself by not taking the burden of proof seriously, etc. Here the speaker is violating social norms, not communicative presuppositions.

(c) Lies, too, do not damage the internal organization of speech as long as they occur as openly declared and permissible components of strategic action. Only if they are used to disguise a conflict can they distort communication. But in that case it is not the presupposition of truth but that of sincerity that is violated: the speaker is not expressing her intention sincerely; she *knows* that her statement is false, but hides it from others.

The comparison of these examples shows that communication can be systematically distorted only if the internal organization of speech is disrupted. This happens if the validity basis of linguistic communication is curtailed *surreptitiously;* that is, without leading to a break in communication or to the transition to openly declared and permissible strategic action. The validity basis of speech is curtailed surreptitiously if at least one of the three universal validity claims to intelligibility (of the expression), sincerity (of the intention expressed by the speaker), and normative rightness (of the expression relative to a normative background) is violated and communication nonetheless continues on the presumption of *communicative* (not strategic) action oriented toward reaching mutual understanding. This is only possible by splitting communication, by doubling it up into a public and a private process. We can examine how this happens by further looking at defense mechanisms. Since systematically distorted communication continues the thread of action oriented to reaching understanding, this disturbance may be culturally normalized under certain conditions. The confounding thing about "systematic distortion" is that the same validity claims that are being violated (and violation of which has pathological effects) at the same time serve to keep up the appearance of consensual action. The violation of the transcendental presupposition of *cognition* has the effect of a loss of meaning, as can be seen in the example of category mistakes. The violation of the transcendental presuppositions of *communication* also leads to a loss of meaning, if the speaker falls below the level of differentiation of the second level of communication (as is the case with schizophrenic linguistic disturbances). But these are extreme cases. Usually communicative pathologies result not in a loss of meaning, but in distortion. This is because communicative processes continue as long as the violation of some of their transcendental presuppositions is not manifest, that is, as long as it is not recognized and admitted by the participants.

(4) Systematically distorted communications express a potential for conflict that cannot be completely suppressed but is not supposed to become manifest. On the one hand, the structure of communication is deformed under the pressure of conflicts that are not carried out because the validity basis of speech is damaged. On the other hand, and simultaneously, this deformed structure stabilizes a context of action that, although charged with the potential for conflict, constrains and to some extent immobilizes that potential. Thus we are dealing with conflicts that can be neither openly carried out nor resolved consensually, but that smolder on with the effect of distorting communication.

Conflicts of identity that arise from the unconscious repression of threats to group or ego identity fit this description. An identity can be secured only by means of interpersonal relationships; it stands and falls with the "recognition" it finds—be it at the cross-cultural or international level or at the interpersonal level among friends and family, and so on. If an identity is threatened by the withholding of recognition, it is often defended in a paradoxical manner. On the one hand, every defense is a strategic action; it can be optimized only under the maxims of purposive action. On the other hand, the goal of the defense cannot be attained strategically, that is, by winning a fight or a game by defeating one's opponent—recognition ultimately cannot be won by force. Only disingenuous or apparent recognition can be thus gained; this is either transformed into real recognition or it becomes frail. That is, it becomes clear that the forced signs of recognition were not seriously meant as recognition.

In what follows I want to set aside problems of collective identity and consider defense strategies for personal identities. Laing's observations are helpful here:

A person's "own" identity cannot be perfectly abstracted from his identity-for-others. His identity-for-himself; the identity that others ascribe to him; the identities that he attributes to them; the identity or identities he thinks they attribute to him; what he thinks they think he thinks they think. . . . "Identity" is that whereby one feels that one is *the same* in this place, this time as at that time and at that place, past or future. It is that by which one is identified. I have the impression that most people tend to come to feel that they are the same continuous being from womb to tomb. And that this "identity," the more it is phantasy, is the more intensely defended.[11]

The paradox that I mentioned can be corroborated by the strategies used to defend one's ego identity. The defender, who can stabilize his threatened identity only by succeeding in having it reconfirmed, on the one hand must stand his ground in a conflict, but on the other hand must suppress this conflict in order not to destroy the consensual foundation of the mutually desired recognition and in order not to risk the breakdown of the communicative relationship. At this point, I want to illustrate the dynamics of such identity conflicts with an example that Laing and his colleagues construe as follows.

[The vicious circle] starts to whirl something like this:

Peter:	*Paul:*
1. I'm upset.	1. Peter is upset.
2. Paul is acting very calm and dispassionate.	2. I'll try to help him by remaining calm and just listening.
3. If Paul cared about me and wanted to help he would get more involved and show some emotion also.	3. He's getting even more upset. I must be even more calm.
4. Paul knows that this upsets me.	4. He's accusing me of hurting him.
5. If Paul knows that this behaviour upsets me, then he must be intending to hurt me.	5. I'm really trying to help.
6. He must be cruel and sadistic. Maybe he gets pleasure out of it, etc.	6. He must be projecting.

Attributions of this kind, based on a virtually inextricable mix of mismatched expectations and phantasy and perception, are the very stuff of interhuman reality. One has, for instance, to enter into this realm in order to understand how one person's attributions about others may begin to be particularly disturbing and disjunctive to these others, and come to be repeatedly invalidated by them, so that he may begin to be subject to the global attribution of being mad.[12]

The *first* precondition for this kind of spiraling in interpersonal relationships is a mistrust on the part of at least one party, which can be traced back to insecurity regarding one's own identity. I'm not talking about some arbitrary affect, but about a type of mistrust that can be conceived in terms of the theory of communication: a mistrust of the soundness of the consensual foundation of the interaction, that is, the worry that the other might leave the foundation of action oriented to mutual understanding and might "veer off" more or less surreptitiously into strategic behavior. The *second* precondition of the communicative spiral is a latent lack of agreement in the assessment of (at least one of) the two self-images that regulate the participants' representations of self. In our example the violations of the claims to sincerity and to rightness are relevant for the communicative disturbance.

The first "misunderstanding" appears in the second sequence: Peter does not understand that Paul wants to help him, because Peter expects Paul to behave differently toward him if he wanted to help. The second misunderstanding emerges in the third sequence: Paul does not understand that Peter misunderstands him because he expects Peter to interpret his behavior as helpful. In the fourth sequence, the consensual foundation of the interaction breaks down without either of the participants clearly giving notice that he is abandoning communicative action: Peter believes that Paul intentionally wants to hurt him, while Paul this time knows what Peter means. In the fifth and sixth sequences, both parties reach the conclusion that the other is violating sincerity claims: Peter thinks that Paul is enjoying hurting him, but does not admit it; Paul thinks that Peter is falsely transferring the hostile feelings he has toward Paul onto Paul. Thus Peter attributes to Paul an intentional violation of the claim to sincerity, and Paul attributes to Peter an unintentional one. On the condition—and this is the *third* precondition—that neither of the two partners is in a position to go on acting with an orientation to reaching mutual understanding at a metacommunicative level, the communicative spiral continues.

Let's assume that, in a certain context, our point of departure, namely, Peter's being upset, represents Peter's attempt to assert his identity. Then the systematically generated and reinforced misunderstanding has the paradoxical result of making Peter's identity still less secure. For Peter fails to have his identity, which is represented in his upset response, recognized. The recognition would have to consist in an agreement [*Einverständnis*] that would have given Peter *the feeling* that Paul had *understood* him. Understanding [*Verstehen*], being understood, and feeling to have been understood are functions of a process of reaching understanding, which in this case would have to come about not only by means of (a) the intelligibility of the expression (of Peter's being upset) and (b) the truth of a proposition (equivalent to a nonverbal expression), but also by means of (c) the rightness of Paul's response (calm listening) with reference to a normative context (Peter's and Paul's self-images) and by means of (d) the sincerity of the intentions Peter and Paul express. In the interactive sequences of our example, the requirements (c) and (d) are not met, but communication is nonetheless neither broken off in a manifest change of attitude to strategic action nor continued at the metacommunicative level of a clarificatory discourse. For this reason, this sequence of utterances is an example of systematically produced misunderstandings.

Systematically distorted communication that results from problems of securing ego identity occurs not exclusively but particularly frequently *within family relations*. The family is a privileged site of identity management, not only for children who are only just establishing their identity, but also for adult family members. In addition, this milieu obliges family members to action that is thoroughly oriented to mutual understanding; in societies of our sort, in any case, strategic action is incommensurable with the commitments to consensus that hold within the family. The family regulates informal relationships and intimate face-to-face interactions within the framework of a diffuse structure of roles. Recent literature on ego psychology proceeds from the assumption that interpersonal relationships of this sort always have a *dual character:* "Object relations" serve both the formation and confirmation of a projection of one's identity and the satisfaction of drives. Interpersonal relations within the family are channels of an affective as well as a cognitive exchange, which are determined simultaneously by the psychodynamics of satisfying drives and of securing one's identity. These aspects can be separated only analytically. The diffuse role structure of the nuclear family meets the dual character of the interpersonal relationships that are permitted within it halfway. With respect to the personality systems of its members, the family does not have particularly strong functional specifications. It allows for a broad spectrum of needs to be met. There are no particularly rigid standards for how relationships between family members are defined; the leeway for individual self-presentation is relatively wide since any given aspect of a relationship can be thematized at any time. If, of course, individual family members use a role structure that is subject to conflict simultaneously for satisfying their drives and for securing their identities, special regulatory capacities are called for in order to resolve emerging systemic problems adequately, that is, without recourse to strategies of repression that have oppressive side effects.

Two systemic problems arise from the perspective of the functions that the family system is to fulfill for individual members: optimal need satisfaction and securing identity. A third systemic problem arises from the complementary point of view of what the interactions between members are to achieve for the family system: securing autonomy within the self-regulation of the family's exchange with its surroundings (its "environments"). Moreover, we may assume that the fourth systemic problem, which establishes the family's functional relation to the system of the whole of society, namely, the socialization of the children, can be resolved to the extent that the other three systemic problems can be satisfactorily dealt with. Hence I shall confine myself in what follows to these three.

First, I want to correlate the systemic problems with the dimensions in which their solutions can be analyzed. It will then become clear which of these dimensions is relevant to the external organization of speech and how the pressure of unsolved problems (by means of an unconscious repression of conflicts) has a distorting effect when it is shifted onto the internal organization of speech.

The systemic problem of need satisfaction of individual family members can be examined in the dimension of a *mutual giving and taking*. Processes in this dimension can in turn be examined from three points of view: (a) what the ratio of drive satisfaction to desire frustration is for an individual and how the balance of gratification is distributed among family members; (b) what the proportion of their share of immediate gratifications is relative to delayed gratifications; and (c) how the stimulating variation of stimuli and the stabilizing continuity of stimuli balance out. H. Stierlin has shown that these three dimensions vary independently of one another.[13] The problem of *securing one's identity* can be broken down into three dimensions: (a) the regulation of the proximity and distance that is to be maintained during interactions between participants; (b) the distribution among group members of opportunities to actively take the initiative or simply to experience the activities of others passively; and (c) the degree of convergence and difference between normative orientations, especially between intersubjectively recognized self-images. The problem of the *independence of the family system* from its environment, finally, is a question of boundaries: the extent to which the family closes itself off or opens up, how much it constitutes a unit with regard to family issues and myths, or the extent to which its internal communicative networks are tied to extrafamilial forces.

Empirical studies have shown that a family's ability to solve the above problems stands in an inverse relation to its internal potential for conflict. The latter in turn is a function of the *distribution of power.* The more unequally power is distributed among the (adult) members of a family, the higher the probability of an asymmetrical distribution of the chances each individual has of attaining a satisfactory balance of gratifications.[14] The resulting conflicts, however, often cannot be carried out strategically within the confines of the family because they are immediately intertwined with the identity management of the participants. A family whose power constellations do not permit a solution of the problem of balancing need satisfaction among its members constrains the leeway for successfully managing identities. Ferreira has compared the problem-solving behavior of clinically unusual family groups of three and four members with corresponding behavior of control groups. As expected, the symptomatic families demonstrated a greater potential for conflict (i.e., less spontaneous agreement of attitudes measured prior to family discussions). They needed more time to reach decisions in family discussions, and the satisfaction of drives, measured by the mutual sensitivity toward the wishes of other family members, was lower than in the control families.[15]

Since the 1960s, various theoretical approaches have produced empirical studies of conflict-ridden families. The results cannot easily be reduced to a common denominator.[16] Nevertheless, they warrant several tentative conclusions about the causes of systematically distorted communication. Disturbances of communication in the sense of recurring, structurally produced unclarities and misunderstandings occur more often in families that harbor a "clinical potential" in the broad sense—families, in other words, that have characteristics that count as "symptoms" according to the usual vague preconception of the term. Symptomatic families of this sort are characterized by an asymmetrical distribution of power, with dominance relations and coalition formations, as well as by corresponding tensions, discrepant expectations, reciprocal deprecation, and so on. The conflicts at issue here tend to be smoldering, partially concealed ones that cannot be publicly played out because the psychodynamic preconditions do not exist for reaching an understanding metacommunicatively and dealing with these conflicts discursively. Communicative styles that mediate distance and clear the ground for discourse, such as joking, irony, and forms of trivializing and neutralizing, are therefore also encountered less often in these families. The potential for conflict affects the external organization of speech so as to make likely extreme manifestations in the above-mentioned dimensions. Concepts such as pseudo-mutuality, schism, skew, separatedness, and connectedness that have been developed by research in schizophrenia are not sufficiently precise for our dimensions. They have been selected as counter-concepts to the symmetries of a balanced role systems (role-reciprocity, complementarity of expectation, mutuality of understanding, etc.) and hence they cut across the aspects I want to distinguish in what follows.

Proximity/Distance
The well-known studies of Lidz and Wynne's research teams confirm that the distances between individual family members in pathological families cannot be regulated appropriately. The basic roles of the family (gender/generation) either are too separated from one another or remain too diffuse, so that the boundaries between generations and genders remain overly rigid or insufficiently differentiated. This pattern can permeate all interactions. Thus social distances cannot be implemented as flexible either because the disintegration of the group would lead to splintering and alienation or because a coerced and frantic overintegration would lead to a solidarity that is maintained by force. The concept of apparently maintained reciprocity (pseudo-mutuality) belongs in this context.[17]

Equality/Difference
Hess and Handel have shown how important it is for the family system to allow an appropriate leeway for the self-presentation of indi-

vidual members. In pathological families the mutually corroborated congruence of self-images (i.e., of the represented and recognized identities of members) is either so high that overpowering family stereotypes impede the formation of individuals or so low that the collective unit is threatened by the lack of normative agreement. What is decisive here is neither the degree of stereotyping nor the degree of discrepancy as such, but rather the inability to synthesize aspects of sameness and difference. Thus the need arises to mask the contrast between tolerated self-images and actual behavior.[18]

Activity/Passivity
The unequal distribution of power means that the sphere of action of a partner in interaction is not merely delimited by the sphere of action of another family member, but is determined and controlled by the initiatives of that family member. In symptomatic families, we can often observe patterns of interaction becoming solidified. These ingrained patterns can be traced to the dependence of one spouse on another and to the formation of coalitions between at least one parent and one or several children.[19] U. Oevermann has developed the concept of affective solidarity between parents, which is applicable in this context and is damaged in the families that were studied. Once again, it is not the unequal distribution of activities among family members as such that is the problem, but rather the more or less surreptitiously habitualized dominance relations that prohibit showing any consideration for the desires of marginalized family members. This is a precondition of the various strategies of exploitation internal to the family to which we shall return.

Demarcation of the family system
A large number of observations support the assumption that symptomatic families do not develop a sufficient capacity for self-regulation in order to regulate their exchange with their environment autonomously. Severely dysfunctional families are on the one hand more isolated, they have less well-organized contacts to their surroundings than normal families; but on the other hand, they are less protected from external influences, typically on the part of the parents' two extended families. Ackerman and Behrens have developed

the following typology based on clinical observations. They distinguish, among other things, between the externally isolated family, the family that is externally integrated but not internally unified, and finally, the disintegrated and regressive family.[20] In this context, we can apply the concept of the "rubber fence" that was developed by the Wynne group. The idea is that of a diffuse demarcation of the pathological family, which allows neither for a clear inside-outside differentiation nor, in particular, for a distinction between particularistic and more strongly universalistic relationships. This has the result that family members actually isolate themselves from their environment.

Symptomatic families frequently show extreme readings in the four mentioned dimensions. This means that the interactive and role structures that determine the external organization of speech are too rigid to produce the flexible relation between proximity and distance, between equality and difference, between action initiatives and behavioral responses, between inside and outside, which, according to all empirical indicators are required for the development [*Entwurf*] and maintenance of the ego identity of family members and of the collective identity of the group. The management of the identities of individual members is curtailed in these families. This causes communicative action to be overburdened with the kinds of conflicts that play themselves out in a systematic distortion of communication. *The pressure of identity conflicts is shifted onto the internal organization of speech where it is stabilized but remains unresolved.* This explains the frequent occurrence of communicative disturbances in symptomatic families.

These disturbances are revealed in a thinly veiled strategic use of the means of communication in situations where the consensual basis of communicative action must nonetheless not be abandoned. I am tracing systematically produced unclarities and misunderstandings to the paradoxical achievement of trying to maintain an endangered background consensus, which rests on the reciprocal recognition of validity claims raised in speech acts, precisely by tacitly violating one or several of these universal claims.

(5) In conclusion, I would like to cite some examples of systematically distorted communication. I am using the results of research by

Luc Kaufmann as well as by U. Oevermann and Y. Schütze. Kaufmann[21] analyzes the first fifteen minutes of interviews between a hospitalized patient, the patient's family, and two physicians. There are seven cases of neuroses and depression, seven borderline cases, and seven cases of schizophrenia. The study follows a code plan based on criteria from Wynne and Singer on the one hand and from the Bateson group on the other. Oevermann and Schütze use taped protocols from five visits each with two families; in both cases, the parents have sought counseling because of problems with their children who had just started school. The scenes on which the analysis is based have been selected partly at random, partly based on their relevance for the suspected family conflict. The material is reconstructed at the three levels of speech acts (propositional content, speaker intention, and meaning of interpersonal relations) with a view to how the underlying family conflict is at the same time expressed and concealed in the linguistic medium. I don't want to present the detailed results of the two studies, but will rather draw on them in order to illustrate my account of linguistic disturbances.

Recall that my basic hypothesis is that families in which skewed power constellations, unequally distributed opportunities of need satisfaction, and conflicts threaten cohesiveness tend toward a dedifferentiation or consolidation of interactive and role structures. This signifies an inflexible external organization of speech, which limits the possibilities of individual family members to develop and to maintain their ego identities without mistrust. However, unless the consensual basis of communicative action is manifestly upset (which would make identity conflicts insoluble), identity conflicts can be contained only by diverting the pressure caused by the problem from the external to the internal organization of speech. The distorting effect of flawed communication is explained by the fact that the family consensus *appears* to be maintained. This *pseudo-consensus* is attained at the expense of redeeming the universal validity claims of intelligibility, sincerity, and normative rightness on which the recognition of the background consensus of a successful language game depends. What must not become manifest is the systematic distortion of the validity claims. Communicative disturbances are all the more conspicuous, the more difficult it is to hide the violation of validity claims. I want to distinguish accordingly the following levels at which a pseudo-consensus can be produced:

(a) At the first level, there are strategies to shield the consensus so that the validity basis—which, if examined, would not be subject to consensus—cannot even be sufficiently precisely identified. This can be achieved by using harmless techniques such as breaking off one's own utterances or interrupting someone else. A somewhat more obvious strategy is to ignore the utterances of another or to force a change of topic. Kaufmann distinguishes the following variants of not responding, where (ii)–(v) function as substitutes for a real answer:

(i) simple refusal to answer, i.e., silence;

(ii) answering to someone other than the person asking the question;

(iii) commenting, in the third person, on the person expecting an answer;

(iv) curatorial answer: C answers instead of B to a question or remark by A;

(v) answer or intervention the content of which has nothing to do with what has been said.[22]

The "tangential response," which is an evasive response strategy that imperceptibly shifts the topic by picking up on peripheral elements of the meaning of what has been said (Ruesch) also belongs in this last category. Most conspicuous are strategies of obfuscation: diffuse chatter, spinning tales, sequences that Kaufmann has encoded as "idle communication" [*Leerlaufkommunikation*] (pp. 84ff.) and that Y. Schütze discusses under the heading of redundancy strategies. One repeats and elaborates the details to such an extent that one's interlocutor loses the thread of the conversation and no longer knows what it is about. This gives rise to functional imprecisions and unclarities that do not result from a violation of any specific validity claim, but rather counteract all attempts to examine the status of the agreement more closely and to pursue any suspicion of pseudo-consensus. Typical of this is the "tandem phenomenon" that Kaufmann observed, so named after the two-seat bicycles where you also can't tell who is really "working." The maneuver causes insecurity with regard to role distribution, and individual initiative, authority and responsibility. Thus we cannot tell from the behavior of two people, for example, whether *A* really shares and actively supports *B*'s opinion or whether *A* is only passively "coasting" in the same direction.[23]

(b) At the second level, there are strategies for bringing about a pseudo-consensus. Kaufmann has studied these pseudo-confirmations following Wynne.

A difference of opinion is formulated in the answer or other response as an agreement or, conversely, agreement is reciprocated with divergence. We distinguish between different degrees and variants of pseudo-confirmation: Answers that, because of a hesitation, a particular choice of words, or tone of voice leave a doubt whether the speaker accepts the message of the other as valid or whether he has already disqualified it (easy, frequent disqualification). "Correction" of the sender's message by adding words or sounds that question the value and significance of the sender's communication or simply annul what has been said. "False reciprocation," a common phenomenon where the response is reciprocated in a different "currency" or "coin"; the respondent does not encounter the interlocutor's message at the same (logical) level or does not respond to it with reference to the same context. The false reciprocation practically always represents a disturbance of "interpersonal logic" and can overlap with the phenomenon of paradoxical communication. Pseudo-confirmations, finally, leave out ("forget") some crucial bit of what the other has communicated and operate as though the remainder were the whole. Moreover, the above-mentioned tangentialization may function as a pseudo-confirmation.[24]

The examples that Kaufmann analyzes in what follows show that the pseudo-confirmation disqualifies the complementary speech act at the level of its claims to intelligibility, sincerity, or rightness. At the same time, it suggestively implies that *other* validity claims, which the speaker has not raised at all, are recognized in the speech act. The more or less obvious maneuver thus consists in producing a consensus about speaker intentions and about a normative context that conceals the dissensus about what has actually been said.

(c) At the third level, there are inconsistencies that betray the unavowed violations of the validity claims that underlie the consensus. All inconsistencies impede the intelligibility of utterances; yet under certain circumstances, they can be traced back to the fact that the speaker deceives herself or others about her intentions or presupposes the intersubjective recognition of what is in fact a disputed normative context. I would like to disregard extreme linguistic errors such as bizarre or idiosyncratic sentence constructions, obviously incorrect pronunciation, concretistic concept formation, category mistakes, secret messages in telegram style, onomatopoeic associations, nonstandard plays on words, mannerisms, etc., which indicate that a speaker is operating below the level of differentiation of normal speech. In the present context, what is of interest are the less obvious divergences that are produced specifically by violating logical, semantic, and pragmatic rules and that threaten the pseudo-consensus from the outset through an alienating unintelligibility.

Conversational sequences that do not hang together logically are usually the result of self-contradictions,

namely in the form of parts of or additions to communication that diminish, devalue, or render questionable the whole of the communication; "forgetting" what has or has been said in the course of the same communication by the same person or of what has not been said, but is obviously being presup posed; all those individual communications that, to the ear of the examiner, contain a partial retraction of what has been said.[25]

Logical incoherence may be the manifestation of a peculiar strategy that Y. Schütze describes as follows:

One associates a loose chain of arguments that cannot be rendered logically consistent, that is, one uses an argument, withdraws its assertoric force in the next step of the argument, and uses it in another context such that it now has a new meaning, which is the opposite of how it was used initially.[26]

The incoherence does not arise from a logical incompetence, mistaken inferences or definitions, but rather from the readiness subsequently to disqualify validity claims that one initially defended. This also applies to the self-contradictory strategy of conditional self-denial: "Concessions are made to the point of self-denial. If the other then believes to have won, one makes an about-face and withdraws or relativizes one's concessions."[27]

The simultaneous expression of two contrary expectations is par-

ticularly confusing. This paradoxical communication has been studied by the Palo-Alto team as the "double-bind." Bateson and his
colleagues of course did not sufficiently differentiate between intentional paradoxes that are used for conveying a message indirectly
and are part of normal linguistic communication and the involuntary paradoxes that stabilize a pseudo-consensus despite a barely re-
pressible conflict in cases where the addressee is emotionally
dependent on the speaker and is unable to verbalize the contradic-
tion, that is, to identify it as such and thus to resolve it (for himself).
Also at the level of logic, there are phenomena of unclear reference
so that no unequivocal attribution of the expressed intensions to particular participants emerges from the course of the conversation. Violations of semantic and pragmatic rules, for example, using words
with idiosyncratic meanings or in a way that is not context-specific,
disregarding presuppositions, and so on, all belong to the realm of
private language utterances. Lorenzer has accounted for these components of private language by means of the mechanism of splitting
the meanings of traumatic scenarios from public language use, that
is, by means of the process of desymbolization.[28] This concept fits our
model, for the private meanings, on this interpretation, express the
unlicensed speaker intention so that they cannot endanger the existing superficial consensus owing to their unintelligibility.

This survey of typical patterns of systematically distorted communication was to give a preliminary illustration of the suggested concept of a communicative disturbance at the level of the validity basis
of speech. I have tried to explain the overburdening of the internal
organization of speech in terms of the pressure exerted by problems
that stem from conflicts of identity and that initially overtax the external organization of speech. Yet merely saying that the pressure exerted by these problems is "shifted" or "diverted" to the internal
organization of speech where it is "absorbed" does not explain
much. We can only understand this process if we follow its intrapsychic traces and clarify how unconscious defense mechanisms
against conflicts work and intervene in communicative action. However, conflicts of identity, on the one hand, and the distorted communicative structures within which such conflicts smolder, on the

other, are part of a circular process. The conflicts, as it were, cause the systematic distortion, yet can be traced back to deficiencies of ego organization (in the parents' generation), which in turn were produced in deviant formative processes, that is, in families with distorted communicative structures. Simplistic assumptions about diffusion and transmission are inadequate for fully grasping the intergenerational transmission of communicative and identity disturbances. This requires clarification in at least three domains of hypotheses: I have in mind the developmental problems that are specific to the levels of a biphasic formative process; a classification in terms of developmental logic of the pathologies that are caused by (or are corollaries of) unfavorable conditions of socialization; and, lastly, an etiology that accounts for the connection between communicative disturbances within the family and childhood pathologies.

Notes

Translator's Introduction

1. Jürgen Habermas, *The Theory of Communicative Action*, 2 vols., trans. Thomas McCarthy (Boston: Beacon Press, 1984/1987). Hereafter cited as TCA.

2. For the sake of convenience, I shall refer to them henceforth as the Gauss Lectures. They follow closely upon the publication of the English translation of *Knowledge and Human Interest*, trans. Jeremy J. Shapiro (Boston: Beacon Press, 1971), and more or less coincide with the 1970 German publication of *On the Logic of the Social Sciences*, trans. Shierry Weber Nicholsen and Jerry A. Stark (Cambridge, MA: MIT Press, 1988).

3. The fourth lecture clearly served as basis for the essay "What Is Universal Pragmatics?" trans. Thomas McCarthy, in *Communication and the Evolution of Society* (Boston: Beacon, 1979), pp. 1–68.

4. See John Searle, *Speech Acts* (Cambridge, England: Cambridge University Press: 1969), 57ff., as well as Jürgen Habermas, "Toward a Critique of a Theory of Meaning," in *Postmetaphysical Thinking*, trans. William Hohengarten (Cambridge, Mass.: MIT Press, 1992), pp. 70–72, and "What Is Universal Pragmatics?" pp. 60–61.

5. Habermas, "What Is Universal Pragmatics?" 13. See also his "Reconstruction and Interpretation in the Social Sciences," in *Moral Consciousness and Communicative Action*, trans. Shierry Weber Nicholsen (Cambridge, Mass.: MIT Press, 1988), pp. 21–42.

6. This dialogical dimension is lacking in Saul Kripke's discussion of the rule-following problem, even though the connection of the private language argument with the rule-following problem is strikingly similar. See Saul Kripke, *Wittgenstein on Rules and Private Language* (Cambridge, Mass.: Harvard University Press, 1982).

7. Robert Brandom, *Making It Explicit* (Cambridge, Mass.: Harvard University Press, 1994).

8. See TCA:1, pp. 295–328.

9. See Cristina Lafont, *The Linguistic Turn in Hermeneutic Philosophy* (Cambridge, Mass.: MIT Press, 1999), chs. 5–6.

10. See Jürgen Habermas, "Rorty's Pragmatic Turn," in *On the Pragmatics of Communication*, ed. Maeve Cooke (Cambridge, Mass.: MIT Press, 1998), pp. 343–382. For his account of discourse ethics, see *Moral Consciousness and Communicative Action*, trans. Christian Lenhardt and Shierry Weber Nicholsen (Cambridge, Mass.: MIT Press, 1990), and *Justification and Application*, trans. Ciarin Cronin (Cambridge, Mass.: MIT Press, 1994). Habermas's critique of empiricist ethics in the essay "On Intentions, Conventions, and Linguistic Interactions" offers insight into the roots of his fundamentally intersubjectivist approach to ethics. See pp. 118–125 in this volume.

11. Cf. "What Is Universal Pragmatics?" pp. 35 and 54.

12. Jürgen Habermas, *Zur Logic der Sozialwissenschaften* (Frankfurt: Suhrkamp, 1982), p. 10, and TCA 1: xli.

13. For further changes, see TCA. Subsequent modifications to the theory have often been the result of Habermas's response to his critics. See his replies in J. B. Thompson and D. Held, eds., *Habermas: Critical Debates* (Cambridge, Mass.: MIT Press, 1982), Richard Bernstein, ed., *Habermas and Modernity* (Cambridge, Mass.: MIT Press, 1985), and Axel Honneth and Hans Joas, eds., *Communicative Action* (Cambridge, Mass.: MIT Press, 1992).

14. See Jürgen Habermas, "Toward a Critique of a Theory of Meaning," in *Postmetaphysical Thinking*, trans. William M. Hohengarten (Cambridge, Mass: MIT Press, 1992).

15. See "Some Further Clarifications of the Concept of Communicative Rationality," in *On the Pragmatics of Communication*. Here Habermas distinguishes communicative use of language from epistemic and teleological use.

16. A dialogue between the two has already been initiated. See Jürgen Habermas, "Von Kant zu Hegel: Zu Robert Brandoms Sprachpragmatik," in *Wahrheit und Rechtfertigung* (Frankfurt: Suhrkamp, 1999), pp. 138–185. An English translation is forthcoming in *The European Journal of Philosophy*.

Lecture I

1. [Although he assigns primacy to linguistic meaning, Habermas conceives of *Sinn* quite broadly. He does not distinguish in these lectures between "sense" (*Sinn*) and "reference" (*Bedeutung*) in the tradition of Frege, for example, as his point of departure is not that tradition but social action theory, where "meaning" is the usual term. Trans.]

2. Cf. John Searle, *Speech Acts* (Cambridge: Cambridge University Press, 1969), pp. 19ff.

3. Cf. D. S. Shwayder's conceptual analyses in his *The Stratification of Behavior* (London: Routledge & Kegan Paul, 1965).

4. Cf. A. V. Cicourel, *Method and Measurement in Sociology* (New York: Free Press, 1964).

5. H. G. Gadamer, *Truth and Method*, 2nd rev. ed. (New York: Crossroad, 1989).

6. N. Malcolm, "Intentional Activity Cannot be Explained by Contingent Causal Laws," in L. I. Krimerman, ed., *The Nature and Scope of Social Science* (New York: Appleton-Century-Crofts, 1969), 334–350; Th. Mishel, *Psychologische Erklärungen* (Frankfurt: 1981).

7. Cf. N. Chomsky's critique of Skinner in J. A. Fodor and J. J. Katz, eds., *The Structure of Language* (Englewood Cliffs: Prentice-Hall, 1964), 547–578.

8. Cf. Krimerman, *Nature and Scope of Social Science*, Part 7, pp. 585ff., especially the articles by Watkins, Goldstein, and Mandelbaum.

9. Ibid., p. 604.

10. Ibid., p. 605.

11. Peter L. Berger and Thomas Luckmann, *The Social Construction of Reality* (Garden City, N.Y.: Doubleday, 1966).

12. G. Simmel, *Soziologie* (Leipzig: Duncker & Humbolt, 1908; 3rd ed, 1923). [A partial translation appears as "How Is Society Possible?" in *On Individuality and Social Forms*, ed. Donald Levine (Chicago: University of Chicago Press, 1971), pp. 6–22. Where appropriate, references to the English are included in square brackets. Trans.]

13. Ibid., p. 22 [p. 6, translation modified].

14. Ibid., p. 22 [p. 7].

15. Ibid., p. 23 [p. 8].

16. Ibid., p. 24.

17. Ibid., p. 23.

18. In comparison with Rickert's and Dilthey's proposals for a theory of the cultural or human sciences, Simmel's brief comments are merely programmatic. On the other hand, this program derives immediately form Kant and, unlike the theories of Rickert and Dilthey, does not aim to provide a foundation for the human sciences that developed in the nineteenth century. Instead, it is geared toward a constitutive social theory in the strict sense. The only one who pursued a similar goal and actually went through with an epistemological foundation of the social sciences is Max Adler in *Das Rätsel der Gesellschaft* (Vienna: Saturn, 1936). More recently, Helmut Schelsky has renewed the call for a "transcendental theory of society"; see his *Ortsbestimmung der deutschen Soziologie* (Düsseldorf: E. Diederich, 1959), 93ff. His empirical work, however, belongs more to an anthropological theory of society. Thus the subjectivist approaches in contemporary sociology all derive directly (Schütz, Berger, Luckmann, Nathanson) or indirectly (Garfinkel, Cicourel, Sacks) from Husserl rather than from Kant. Rickert's philosophy of value of course has found its way into more recent sociology via Max Weber and Parsons. However, the constitutive problem already receded into the background in Weber, and in Parsons it was superceded by the basic tenets of a moderately empiricist philosophy of science.

Lecture II

1. Edmund Husserl, *The Crisis of European Sciences and Transcendental Phenomenology*, trans. D. Carr (Evanston, IL: Northwestern University Press, 1970), §28ff., pp. 103ff. Hereafter cited as *Crisis*.

2. *Crisis*, §32, p. 119.

3. *Crisis*, §51, p. 173.

4. Husserl reproaches Kant for the "lack of an intuitive exhibiting method" (*Crisis*, §30, p. 114).

5. Simmel apparently fails to see the inherent difficulty of the architectonic of the Kantian opus. Max Adler, in contrast, undertakes the following revision. He introduces the social *a priori* and raises this relationship of the singular ego to the community of many egos to the level of the transcendental determination of the individual consciousness: "Transcendental epistemology not only teaches that every object necessarily belongs to a subject, but much more: to be an object is for the thing to belong to indeterminately many subjects. This plurality must not be understood empirically, but transcendentally, that is, already as characteristic of the individual consciousness itself." Adler, *Das Rätsel der Gesellschaft* (Vienna: Saturn, 1936), p. 111.

6. In connection with what follows, see Ernst Tugendhat's excellent study on the concept of truth in Husserl and Heidegger: *Der Wahrheitsbegriff bei Husserl und Heidegger* (Berlin: De Gruyter, 1967), part 1.

7. Edmund Husserl, *Ideas Pertaining to a Pure Phenomenology and to a Phenomenological Philosophy*, book 1, trans. F. Kersten (The Hague: Martinus Nijhoff, 1982), §24, p. 44.

8. *Ideas*, §30, pp. 56ff.

9. *Crisis*, §40, p. 149.

10. *Ideas*, §117, p. 279.

11. *Ideas*, §116, p. 277.

12. Edmund Husserl, "Meditation über die Idee eines individuellen und Gemeinschaftslebens in absoluter Selbstverantwortung" and "Besinnung als Aktivität," both in *Husserliana*, ed. (The Hague: Marinus Nijhoff, 1959), pp. 193–211.

13. Ibid., p. 194.

14. Ibid., p. 197.

15. Ibid., p. 199.

16. Vico's epistemic interpretation of the phrase *factum et verum convertuntur,* which he develops based on the model of geometry, is based on this insight.

Notes

17. For a critique of immediacy as a concept of epistemological justification, see T. W. Adorno, *Zur Metakritik der Erkenntnistheorie* (Stuttgart: Kolhammer, 1956).

18. Edmund Husserl, *Cartesian Meditations*, trans. D. Cairns (The Hague: Martinus Nijhoff, 1960), §49, p. 107.

19. Ibid.

20. Ibid., §55, p. 123.

21. Schütz refers to corresponding works by Scheler, Sartre, and Merleau-Ponty. "The Problem of Transcendental Intersubjectivity in Husserl," in *Collected Papers*, vol. 3, ed. I. Schütz (The Hague: Martinus Nijhoff, 1966), pp. 51–84.

22. Husserl, *Cartesian Meditations*, §52, p. 114. [Translation modified. Trans.]

23. Schütz, "The Problem of Transcendental Intersubjectivity in Husserl," p. 76.

24. *Crisis*, p. 184.

25. "As primal ego, I constitute my horizon of transcendental others as cosubjects within the transcendental intersubjectivity which constitutes the world," ibid.

Lecture III

1. To begin with, I shall eschew the question of how it is possible that the same propositional content can pick out many different things: "If we admit one content 'in' many representings, why not admit one attribute 'in' many things: platonism for things as well as platonism for thoughts?" (W. Sellars, *Science and Metaphysics* [London: Routledge and Kegan Paul, 1968], p. 62). Elsewhere, Sellars talks about content as inherent in [*Innewohnen*] acts of consciousness (in-esse of attributes in representings) and of content residing within things themselves (in-esse of attributes in things) (p. 92).

2. Sellars, *Science and Metaphysics*, p. 62.

3. I am disregarding the fact that Sellars from the outset interprets acts of consciousness objectivistically, that is, as mental episodes: "If anything which occurs or takes place is to count as an episode, then, whenever an object changes from having one disposition to having another the change is an episode" (ibid., p. 72). Sellars's physicalism manifests itself in that he conceives of acts of consciousness or representings as events in the world like objectified natural events.

4. Ibid., p. 64: [Sellars proceeds by identifying contents first with intensions and then with (Fregean) senses. This distinction does not figure in Habermas's account here. Trans.]

5. Sellars, *Science and Metaphysics*, p. 156.

6. Ibid.

7. Ibid., p. 76.

8. Ibid., p. 157.

9. Ludwig Wittgenstein, *Philosophical Investigations* (Oxford: Blackwell, 1958), §202, p. 81.

10. [For a similar interpretation of Wittgenstein, see Saul Kripke, *Wittgenstein on Rules and Private Language* (Cambridge, MA: Harvard University Press, 1982). Trans.]

11. Cf. Peter Winch, *The Idea of a Social Science and Its Relation to Philosophy* (London: Routledge & Kegan Paul, 1958), pp. 24–44; also H. J. Giegel, *Die Logic der seelischen Ereignisse* (Frankfurt: Suhrkamp, 1969), pp. 99–108, 112, 134.

12. Sellars, *Science and Metaphysics*, p. 128.

13. E.g., *Philosophical Investigations*, §182, p. 73.

14. *Philosophical Investigations*, §445, p. 131.

15. Ludwig Wittgenstein, *Philosophical Grammar*, trans. A. Kenny (Berkeley: University of California Press, 1974), part I, §111, p. 160.

16. Ibid., Part I, §45, p. 88.

17. Ibid., Part I, §84, p. 131. [Translation modified. Trans.]

18. "No one will deny that studying the nature of the rules of games must be useful for the study of grammatical rules, since it is beyond doubt that there is some sort of similarity between them.—The right thing is to let the instinct that there is a kinship lead one to look at the rules of games without any preconceived judgement or prejudice about the analogy between games and grammar" (ibid., §134, p. 187).

19. Ludwig Wittgenstein, *Philosophical Remarks* (Oxford: Blackwell, 1975), vol. 2, §54, pp. 84ff.

20. *Philosophical Grammar*, part II, §9, p. 272.

21. *Philosophical Investigations*, §206, p. 82.

22. Cf. Jürgen Habermas, *Knowledge and Human Interests*, trans. J. Shapiro (Boston: Beacon Press, 1971), ch. 7, pp. 140–160.

23. *Philosophical Investigations*, §241, p. 88.

24. Ibid., §199, p. 80.

25. *Philosophical Grammar*, part I, §133, p. 184.

26. Ibid., part I, §29, p. 65 [italics J.H.].

27. Ibid., p. 66 [original italics].

28. *Philosophical Investigations*, §142, p. 56.

29. G. H. Mead, *Mind, Self, Society* (Chicago: University of Chicago Press, 1934).

Notes

30. *Philosophical Investigations,* §23, p. 11.

31. [Other Habermas translators, following McCarthy, have rendered *Verständlichkeit* as "comprehensibility." However, "intelligibility" is the more usual in contexts of philosophy of language. Trans.]

Lecture IV

1. Noam Chomsky, *Aspects of a Theory of Syntax* (Cambridge, MA: The MIT Press, 1965), pp. 3ff.

2. Cf. E. H. Lenneberg, *Biological Foundations of Language* (New York: Wiley, 1967).

3. Dieter Wunderlich, *Tempus und Zeitreferenz im Deutschen* (Munich: Hueber, 1970).

4. D. S. Shwayder, *The Stratification of Behavior* (London: Routledge & Kegan Paul, 1965), p. 288.

5. That is, the illocutionary acts analyzed by Searle following Austin and Strawson; see *Speech Acts* (London: Cambridge University Press, 1969).

6. By introducing the singular speech act as the elementary unit of speech, we already perform an abstraction: We prescind from the fact that speech acts usually occur in pairs, as questions and answers, assertions and denials, etc.

7. Even if the performative components are not explicitly verbalized, they are always implicit in the linguistic process. Thus they must be present in the deep structure of *every* linguistic utterance.

8. Dell Hymes uses the expression instead for the mastery of linguistic codes; for this I have suggested the term *pragmatic competence.*

9. In the most recent linguistic debates, consideration of universal pragmatic relations has led to a revision of the semantic theory initially proposed by Katz, Fodor, Postal, and others. In the newer conception of generative semantics, drawing on the work of McCawley, Fillmore, and especially Lakoff, the categorical separation of syntactic deep structure and semantic interpretation for meaning-preserving transformations has been dropped and replaced with the assumption of a semantic deep structure with pre- and postlexical transformations. Accordingly, the process of sentence formation begins with a semantic entity whose general characterization also involves aspects of universal pragmatics. Ross and McCawley have suggested interpreting every highest *S* as a performative utterance, that is, as the dominant clause of a speech act. Lakoff and others incorporate, in addition to the performative mode (question, order, assertion, etc.), references to possible speech situations, as well as focus, presupposition, and co-reference into the description of deep structure. Fillmore's suggestion of representing deep structure as a role structure that would show how elements such as agentives, instrumentals, datives, factitives, locatives, objectives, etc., contribute to sentence meaning approximates a cognitivist approach to semantics. I cannot predict the course of this discussion within linguistics. Nevertheless, there are indications that in describing semantic deep structure, linguistics will come across a linguistically basic system of reference that might be understood as a representation of the rule system of universal pragmatics.

10. Cf. Searle, *Speech Acts,* pp. 29ff.

11. We may call the use of language that exploits this reflexivity for purposes of paraphrasing *hermeneutic.* Relative to the cognitive and communicative uses of language, it occurs at a metalevel, but it is nonetheless an element of everyday communication since it merely expresses the reflexivity inherent in natural language. I do not wish to elaborate on this here.

12. Empiricist pragmatics in the sense of a behaviorist semiotics (Charles Morris), of course, characteristically introduces the universal structures of speech without reference to pragmatic universals from the perspective of the observer. Cf. K. O. Apel, "Szientismus oder transcendental Hermeneutik? Zur Frage nach dem Subject der Zeicheninterpretations in der Semiotik des Pragmatismus," in R. Bubner et al. (eds.), *Hermeneutik und Dialektik* (Tübingen: Mohr, 1970), vol. 1, pp. 105–144; also Arno Müller, *Probleme der behavioristischen Semiotik* (doctoral dissertation, University of Frankfurt, 1970).

13. Searle, *Speech Acts,* pp. 57ff.

14. Austin groups these speech acts with "behabitives" and "exercisives" (see Searle, *Speech Acts,* pp. 150–162).

Lecture V

1. Cf. Wilfrid Sellars, *Science, Perception, and Reality* (New York: Humanities Press, 1963), pp. 100ff.

2. [The German here reads: "wobei '*s*' einen assertorischen Satz mit der Bedeutung '*p*' bezeichnet." In keeping with Frege's distinction between sense (*Sinn*) and reference (*Bedeutung*), Habermas can be understood as saying that *s* has *p* as its *reference.* This interpretation fits well with the subsequent discussion of correspondence theories of truth. The formulation is particularly interesting in light of Davidson's appropriation of Tarski's semantic conception of truth. Davidson explicitly uses Convention T to replace '*means* that.' (See Donald Davidson, "Truth and Meaning," in *Inquiries into Truth and Interpretation* (Oxford: Oxford University Press, 1984).) Trans.]

3. Cf. E. Tugendhat, in *Philosophische Rundschau,* vol. 8, no. 2/3, pp. 131–159.

4. Tugendhat (ibid., p. 138) rightly maintains that "if the meaning of 'true' is exhausted by the fact that we can replace '*p* is true' by '*p*,' then any inquiry into the truth of judgments is pointless."

5. Cf. K. O. Apel's introduction to C. S. Peirce, *Schriften I* (Frankfurt: Suhrkamp, 1968).

6. Cf. H. G. Gadamer, *Truth and Method,* 2nd rev. ed. (New York: Crossroad, 1989), and Karl Popper, *The Logic of Scientific Discovery* (New York: Basic Books, 1959).

7. [For a recent discussion of world disclosure, see *Thesis 11,* vol. 37 (1994), especially the articles by Kompridis, Lafont, Seel, and Bohmann. Trans.]

Notes

8. This difference may be connected with the fact that empirical beliefs must be grounded in experience whereas the acceptance or rejection of norms need not have an immediate experiential connection to external reality. The claim of a norm to be right may be based on the reflexive experience of the participating subjects of themselves. This experience indicates whether one "really wants" to accept the norm and whether the interpretation of needs and desires that it expresses "really" picks out what can be understood as "one's own" needs and desires.

9. S. Toulmin, *The Uses of Argument* (Cambridge: Cambridge University Press, 1964), pp. 146ff.

10. This goal cannot be attained because we cannot go behind a discourse; that is, we cannot engage in "metadiscourse." In a metadiscourse, we act as if—and this has been our attitude until now—we could ascertain that the participants in this discourse satisfy the conditions that allow them to participate in discourse. Yet strictly speaking, discourse and metadiscourse are at the same level. *All* discourses are intersubjective events. The appearance of the arbitrary iteration of the self-reflection of isolated subjects does not so much as get off the ground; see A. Kulenkampff, *Antinomie und Dialektik* (Stuttgart: Metzler, 1970). Even the self-reflection whereby interlocutors ascertain that they have indeed stepped out of contexts of communicative action and have suspended the forces of the reality of making risky decisions—even this is an intersubjective event; cf. my *Knowledge and Human Interests*, trans. J. Shapiro (Boston: Beacon Press, 1971), ch. 10). We cannot engage in discourse without *presupposing* that the conditions for entering into discourse have already been met. After having made this presupposition, however, discourse about whether we were right to do so is meaningless. At the level of discourse, there can be no separation of discourse and the external point of view of observing discourse.

11. I have sought to characterize the ideal speech situation not in terms of the features of the personality of ideal speakers, but in terms of the structural features of a context of possible speech, specifically the symmetric distribution of opportunities to take on dialogue roles and to perform speech acts. This construction is meant to demonstrate that we are indeed *capable* of anticipating an ideal speech situation, which a competent speaker must be able to do if she wants to participate in discourse, by means of the four mentioned classes of speech acts—and only those four. Hence my suggestion for giving a systematic account of speech acts can be justified in retrospect from the point of view that speech acts can only function as pragmatic universals—that is, as means of producing universal structures of possible speech—if they can simultaneously serve for designing an ideal speech situation.

12. Even a discursively justified validity claim regains the status of being "naively" presupposed as soon as the result of the discourse reenters contexts of action.

13. This also holds in the special case of therapeutic discourse, which both interlocutors enter with the intention of raising unconscious motives to the level of consciousness.

14. I have since retracted this formulation. See J. Habermas, "A Reply to my Critics," in J. B. Thompson and D. Held, eds., *Habermas: Critical Debates* (Cambridge, MA: The MIT Press, 1982), pp. 261ff.

Intentions, Conventions, and Linguistic Interactions

1. M. Roche, "Die philosophische Schule der Sprachanalyse," in R. Wiggershaus, ed., *Sprachanalyse und Soziologie* (Frankfurt: Suhrkamp, 1975), p. 187.

2. Ibid., pp. 188ff.

3. Charles Taylor, "Explaining Action," *Inquiry*, 13, 1970, 54–89.

4. R. Norman, *Reasons for Actions* (Oxford: Blackwell, 1971), p. 24.

5. Ibid., pp. 63–64.

6. Ibid., p. 72.

7. From J. Narveson, *Morality and Utility* (Baltimore: Johns Hopkins University Press, 1967), quoted in Norman, *Reasons for Actions*, p. 48.

8. D. S. Shwayder, *The Stratification of Behavior* (London: Routledge & Kegan Paul, 1965), pp. 254ff.

9. See my critique of intentionalist semantics in J. Habermas, "Intentionalistische Semantik," in *Vorstudien und Ergänzungen zur Theorie des kommunikativen Handelns* (Frankfurt: Suhrkamp, 1984). [More recently, Habermas has made this criticism in "Comments on John Searle: Meaning, Communication, and Representation," in *John Searle and His Critics*, ed. Ernest Lepore and Robert Van Gulick (Oxford: Blackwell, 1991), pp. 17–29, and in *Postmetaphysical Thinking*, trans. Bill Hohengarten (Cambridge, MA: The MIT Press, 1992). Trans.]

Reflections on Communicative Pathology

1. G. Devereux, *Normal und Anormal* (Frankfurt, 1974).

2. Ibid., pp. 28ff.

3. Ibid., pp. 44, 46.

4. Ibid., pp. 122ff.

5. Ibid., pp. 119ff.

6. Ibid., p. 86.

7. J. Habermas, *Knowledge and Human Interests*, trans. J. Shapiro (Boston, MA: Beacon Press 1971), ch. 10, and "The Hermeneutic Claim to Universality," in *Contemporary Hermeneutics*, ed. Josef Bleicher (London: Routledge & Kegan Paul, 1980), pp. 181–211.

8. R. A. Spitz, *Vom Säugling zum Kleinkind* (Stuttgart, 1967).

9. Ibid., p. 204.

10. Ibid., pp. 201ff.

11. R. D. Laing, *Self and Others* (New York: Pantheon, 1969), p. 70.

12. R. D. Laing, H. Phillipson, and A. R. Lee, *Interpersonal Perception* (New York: Springer, 1966), pp. 21–22.

13. H. Stierlin, *Das Tun des Einen ist das Tun des Anderen* (Frankfurt: Suhrkamp, 1971).

14. W. D. Winter and A. J. Ferreira, eds., *Research in Family Interaction* (Palo Alto: Science and Behavior Books, 1969).

15. See the literature review in the introduction to L. Kaufmann, *Familie, Kommunikation, Psychose* (Bern: 1972).

16. G. Handel, ed., *The Psychosocial Interior of the Family* (Chicago: Aldine, 1967).

17. E. G. Mishler and N. E. Waxler, *Interaction in Families* (New York: Wiley, 1968).

18. R. D. Hess and G. Handel, "The Family as a Psychosocial Organization," in Handel, *The Psychosocial Interior of the Family*, pp. 10ff.

19. M. T. Siegert, *Strukturbedingungen von Familienkonflikten* (Frankfurt: Suhrkamp, 1977).

20. N. W. Ackerman and M. L. Behrens, "A Study of Family Diagnosis," *American Journal of Orthopsychiatry* (1956): 66ff.

21. Kaufmann, *Familie, Kommunikation, Psychose*, pp. 73ff.

22. Ibid., p. 106.

23. Ibid., pp. 105ff.

24. Ibid., p. 92.

25. Ibid., p. 81.

26. Y. Schütze, *Innerfamiliale Kommunikation und kindliche Psyche* (Berlin, 1977).

27. Ibid.

28. A. Lorenzer, *Sprachzerstörung und Rekonstruktion* (Frankfurt: Suhrkamp, 1970).

Index

Index

progesterone . co. uk